To Jeanette —
Hope you ... little stories ... of experience ... my ... Margaret JJ Ranch

Mar. 2008

The Fine Line

Margaret Watkins

Outskirts Press, Inc.
Denver, Colorado

The Fine Line

Outskirts Press
http://www.outskirtspress.com

ISBN-10: 1-4327-0250-5
ISBN-13: 978-1-4327-0250-2

Library of Congress Control Number: 2006937253

Outskirts Press and the "OP" logo are trademarks belonging to
Outskirts Press, Inc.

Printed in the United States of America

CONTENTS

ACKNOWLEDGMENTS

In the years following my medical meltdown I learned much about aneurysms and the pathways of their destruction. The contents and format of this book have undergone many permutations as I have struggled to present the uniqueness of these parallel stories. I believe that the overlap of events and subsequent reconnections between me and Colonel Robbins did not happen merely by serendipity.

My husband, Robert, planted the seed for this endeavor when he brought a tape recorder to Harborview and encouraged me to talk about my day-to-day tribulations. He coaxed my initial writing of the rough draft for this book paragraph by shaky paragraph. The power of his love helped me to return from my journey into darkness. His patient attention to my reading of the many revisions of each chapter has earned him a gold medal for good conduct.

In Michael Robbins I have found a compatriot and a friend. His diligence in working with me on the manuscript had more to do with our choices of good restaurants than with any literary genius on my part. As we occasionally associate between Minnesota and Idaho

I continue to admire his ability to make lemonade.

Early in my recovery I discovered *A Bomb in the Brain.* I am grateful to Steve Fishman for his courageous book which inspired me to tell these stories.

Selma Lamb and Sheldon Hentschke were there when I needed them. The Rember family was the personification of mountain brotherhood. Miss Betty and Mr. Craig unveiled their love of the Sawtooth Valley and incorporated Robert and me into the fellowship of this rugged mountain society.

Many thanks to Stan Kidwell of Edge Graphics, Boise, Idaho, for transforming my vague ideas into beautiful cover designs.

To Jessica and Hiliary I owe the immeasurable joy of a mother's love.

FOREWORD

ANEURYSM (ăn'yə-rĭz'əm) n. *Pathol.* A permanent cardiac or arterial dilatation usually caused by weakening of the vessel wall (Webster 2001). Aneurysms rupture quickly and without warning. They are silent killers about which much is understood by the medical profession and little is known by the public. These defects may occur anywhere in the human body but have a predilection for the convoluted circulation of the central nervous system.

Cerebral aneurysms are far more prevalent than commonly appreciated. They erupt in some 50,000 Americans each year---one third of whom will die on the spot. One half of the victims surviving the initial hemorrhage will die from complications while hospitalized. Handicaps in the survivors may range from mild neuromuscular dysfunction to irreversible coma.

Aneurysms do not select the weak, the frail, the old. They are not respecters of gender, race, or social status. With minor variations in incidence, every population group in the world will be similarly affected. The numbers are staggering.

The year 2000 population census for the United

States was 281,421,906 citizens. With a very conservative estimate of aneurysms of two per cent, there are currently nearly six million Americans walking around with potential volcanoes inside their heads. In his lifetime, almost every person will be touched by the tragedy of a ruptured aneurysm---parent, sibling, friend, child.

The medical literature is replete with tomes on the subject of aneurysms. There are specialty fields of Neurosurgery and Neuroradiology dedicated solely to the complexities of diagnosing and correcting these devastating anomalies. There is, however, a paucity of information available to the public to increase their awareness of this malady and to offer information and encouragement to those assailed by an aneurysm in their midst.

I believe that *The Fine Line* can serve the dual purpose of informing and inspiring. I strive to explain in a straightforward fashion the pathophysiology of aneurysms and their abysmal track record. My personal saga, combined with Colonel Robbins' story, is a testimonial to both perseverance and faith as well as to the miracle of modern medicine.

Standing in snowshoes on a brilliant winter morning in the high mountains of Idaho, I was broadsided by a ruptured cerebellar aneurysm. Without means to summon help I hunkered down in our cabin for more than two days, expecting death to find me at any moment. My decision to crawl through the snow to the highway for assistance had less to do with heroics than with my persnickety refusal to die without a fight.

The book follows my encounter with the horrors of

brain surgery and the struggles of physical and psychological rehabilitation. I have woven into this story the parallel one of a young fighter jet pilot whose flying career was permanently derailed when an aneurysm laid waste to his life. Suffering our setbacks simultaneously, Colonel Robbins and I were destined to cross paths twice before we became first co-survivors and then friends for life. There was a universal commonness in our suffering and a magic in our healing.

There are many fine lines that separate both major and minor counterbalances in our lives. Death is the final fine line over which we all must ultimately step. My aneurysm ordeal drove me to stand with both feet firmly planted on this line while I surveyed eternity. Colonel Robbins was not far from his own line although he did not fully comprehend that mortality was so near at hand. We are both grateful for the grace that allows us to continue lives that were not yet completed.

In the years since my first rambling attempts to get our stories down on paper, Mike and I have learned of many aneurysm catastrophes. It is our hope that the record of our travails may provide insight and comfort to the survivors of this medical Armageddon or to the families of its victims.

Margaret Watkins
January 1, 2007

.....................I don't know at what point I became aware of the angel. Perhaps it was when I was lying face down on that ugly shag carpet with the mother of all headaches, waiting for my skull to explode.......................

CHAPTER 1

WRAP UP

The telephone rang at the exact moment I walked through the doorway from the garage with a bag of groceries in my arms. I glared at the hateful instrument with open hostility, wishing it would implode into oblivion and take all its unwanted communications with it.

"They are going to do a caesarean section on the mother with triplets at five o'clock. I need your help."

Stewart was a man of few words. His sexy Brooklyn voice betrayed no hint of the emotions he was feeling. On the night shift at the hospital, he would supervise the three teams of medical personnel attending the delivery of these infants born twelve weeks before their due date. Each baby would be roughly the size of a submarine sandwich, less than a foot in length, and would weigh about two pounds. Six

1

tiny arms the size of a man's forefinger. Six little feet smaller than a thumb. Three soft round heads with fine downy coverings of hair called lanugo.

Stewart would be psychologically preparing himself for the onslaught. Based on his extensive past experience, my soon-to-be-besieged partner would be calculating medication doses according to weights suggested by intrauterine ultrasound examination. He would be ordering laboratory and radiological tests with the assumption that the trio would require the highest level of nursing care and the full spectrum of his expertise. And he would be dreading in advance the mountain of paper work to be processed.

"Okay. I'll be there in twenty minutes."

I hung up the phone with a sigh. It was the end of June in 1995, and I had just arrived home from a typical day in the Newborn Intensive Care Unit (NICU) at St. Luke's Regional Medical Center in Boise, Idaho. I had been part of the maternal-child services at St. Luke's for more than fourteen years, serving as medical director of the nurseries for eight of those. The hospital had become my second home.

When I arrived at St. Luke's in 1982, the city of Boise was experiencing an economic boom, and a population explosion was invigorating the southwestern region of Idaho. There were already a dozen prominent corporations headquartered in Boise quietly going about their international businesses. Morrison-Knudsen, Hewlitt-Packard and J. R. Simplot Company of OreIda fame lent their support to the obvious civic pride of the city. One hundred thousand people nestled against the brown foothills and among the mammoth cottonwood trees lining the

Boise River. It seemed to me that St. Luke's should sit up and take notice of all the potential mothers and babies out there. I thought we should expand and upgrade our unit to meet the projected obstetrical and newborn needs. The hospital administration and NICU nursing staff agreed wholeheartedly.

St. Alphonsus Hospital, across town but actually only a ten-minute drive from my hospital, offered specialized services to the public such as trauma and burn units and surgical subdivisions. By tacit agreement Women's Care and Pediatrics were the bailiwicks of St. Luke's, along with matters of the heart and an excellent cancer center. St. Luke's busy maternity service already offered sophisticated medical care. The labor and delivery unit was humming around the clock. Both hospitals were rightfully proud of their areas of specialized medical care.

The "premature nursery" as it was often called, actually took care of a variety of newborn problems, although there was certainly a preponderance of those babies born too early. The premies were placed in sophisticated plastic boxes called isolettes, once known as incubators. They were lined up along walls sprouting a myriad of pipes for oxygen and compressed air and dozens of electrical outlets. The babies' tiny bodies were almost lost in an ocean of digitalized gadgets.

By 1983 it had become obvious that lack of space and outdated equipment would ultimately limit our vision of expansion. We continued to ignore these facts and concentrated on upgrading the skills level and knowledge base of the nursing and support staffs. The personnel eagerly rose to the occasion. We held weekly classes where I educated myself and them on a variety of pertinent topics. Three lectures each Tuesday, with preparation of handouts and audiovisuals, soon caused me to dread the third day of the week. The enthusiasm of the participants helped me to survive the brutal double duty of working and teaching.

We slowly increased our referral area and outreach programs and recruited additional well-trained personnel. The neonatal transport team was rejuvenated by a series of training seminars and a jolt of autonomy. The hospital purchased a fleet of new respirators and radiant warmer beds. The NICU embarked upon a modest remodeling campaign and subtle advertising. Soon we were offering state-of-the-art services to a region covering more than one-hundred-fifty-thousand square miles and including at least thirty hospitals.

For three years I labored alone, assisted in patient care by a small cadre of seasoned pediatricians. The hours were inhumane. The responsibilities were mind-boggling. I began looking for a partner.

Recruitment was a painful process for me. Where would I find another neonatologist willing to work the merciless hours necessary to continue the developmental dream we had initiated? I needed someone to whom I could relinquish care of the patients with absolute certainty that the babies would be looked after with skill and compassion.

My relief came sauntering into town in the form of a young man from Iowa with a killer grin and impeccable credentials. Matthew Sell and I toiled together and pushed the NICU into new quarters and into the technological wizardry of the nineties. Along the way we accumulated a fair number of personal bumps and bruises and two additional associates. The volume of patients continued to expand as did the severity of their illnesses, so that our medical practice remained overworked despite our increased numbers. I still loved my career but the steady drain of physical and emotional reserves took its toll.

It was now fourteen tired years later on a Wednesday afternoon and my retirement from all this excitement was still two long days away. One more night of being on call for disasters. Forty-eight hours until I unclipped the intrusive pager that had permanently adhered to my waist band as the years passed. Just think; no more flinching when the phone rang at mealtimes or when I was in the shower. No more scrabbling around the night stand for receiver and light switch when I was rudely awakened in the middle of the night for a crisis consultation or a frantic rush to the hospital. And my friends and colleagues thought I was going to miss this?

Now, however, I had work to do. Rumors of triplets had been circulating around the nursery for weeks. Now that their arrival was imminent, I felt a surge of the familiar adrenaline rush that always came to me at such times. Over the quarter of a century that I had been attending to the needs of premature and ill infants, I still got a natural high from the controlled chaos of the obstetrical unit in full swing.

My teenaged daughters were nowhere in sight. I threw the perishable foods into the refrigerator and left a note for the children. They were accustomed to being abandoned and would care for themselves. A box of stale cinnamon rolls caught my eye and I grabbed the package on my way through the kitchen to the garage.

I could almost push a button marked HOSPITAL

and have the car take me there automatically. The route around the foothills north of the city was so familiar that I sometimes arrived at St. Luke's having almost no recollection of the drive.

On this trip my thoughts were focused on the mission at hand. A mental checklist of steps for resuscitation ran through my mind unbidden. Even though I had taught countless seminars on the subject, years of training demanded that I review the high-risk-delivery procedures before putting into practice these critical measures.

Since Stewart was in charge of the NICU this week, it would be his call as to my place in the proceedings. I would likely be assigned to the second-born baby, along with a nurse and a respiratory therapist. Together we would ensure that the baby was breathing properly and maintaining good color and heart rate. As is common with multiple gestations, these infants were being born many weeks before term. Certain steps were crucial to keeping them alive. We were called neonatologists because we specialized in the science of the newborn. Nothing thrilled us more than to see a small baby get off to a good start.

When I arrived at the nursery things seemed strangely quiet. Usually there was a great flurry of activity as the NICU staff scurried into assigned positions to facilitate a smooth transition for the new arrivals. This day the personnel seemed remarkably inert. I hoped they were not underestimating the amount of effort soon to be expended. The unit had been thriving on such demanding situations for twenty-five years, so I assumed the relative inactivity reflected their preparedness. They were prepared, all right, but not in the way I imagined!

Ignoring the unexpected inertia in the unit, I went straight to the locker room. Since the resuscitation team entered a sterile operating area, we dressed in the appropriate surgical attire. I emerged from the dressing area in bright blue pants whose cuffs were well above my ankles. An oversized boxy scrub shirt hung off one shoulder. Elasticized paper booties and a white hair net completed my official uniform. Dressed for combat I went in search of my laconic associate to get a status report.

I found Stewart in his usual place, sitting forlornly before the x-ray viewer staring unseeingly at the tiny gray images marching chronologically across the screen. With his chin propped on one palm, he slumped before radiographs of miniature chests, abdomens and skulls. He appeared more morose than when I had last seen him at three o'clock. I clapped a hand firmly on his shoulder and said, "What's up, Stu?" He gave me a withering look.

"In addition to the triplets to deal with," he informed me with doom and gloom, "we also have a critical newborn being transported in from a hospital in eastern Oregon."

Stewart was in an obvious foul mood. Before I could muster much sympathy for my partner the phone rang at the NICU clerk's desk. After an abbreviated conversation, the clerk informed us that the transport team and paramedics were in the emergency room and would soon arrive in the unit. Again I thought it odd that there was a conspicuous lack of the frenetic activity that generally accompanied such an announcement. A strange sort of lethargy seemed to have overcome the place.

I started for the office of the head nurse hoping for some clarification of this unexplained lassitude. The emergency medical technicians came rushing through the double doors into the NICU with a great clatter. It took me a moment to realize that there was no baby isolette on the gurney and no neonatal transport team in attendance.

As I pondered over the unusual nature of this disruptive influx, I felt four sets of strong arms grab my extremities. I was lifted with ease and deposited unceremoniously on the empty stretcher laying on the gurney. Thick Velcro straps soon had me immobilized and within seconds the paramedics were back out of the unit with me in tow. Huge grins on the faces of the hospital personnel confirmed my growing suspicion that the entire nursery crew was up to no good.

We rushed through the emergency ward and into the back of the transport ambulance. With lights flashing and siren blaring we blasted off into the heat of the day. My face was covered with a pillowcase; as if I could see anything, imprisoned as I was on the stretcher which was locked into clamps on the wall of the vehicle. By now I was laughing so hard I was almost in real need of an oxygen mask.

Soon the ambulance screeched to a stop and squelched the siren. When the gurney was wheeled into the shade of a large oak tree I realized that we were in a park. I could hear the subdued murmur of many voices and the laughter of children. As I sat up I was greeted with "Surprise, Dr. Margaret!" from the numerous staff who had gathered with their families for a final picnic in honor of my retirement.

For several hours I held court in my surgical garb like

a medical monarch, saying farewell to friends and colleagues. These people were more than acquaintances and comrades. We had labored together side-by-side administering to the needs of Idaho's most fragile citizens. We had shared laughter and tears, triumph and anguish, successes and failures. This group of noisy exuberant people was my extended family.

Tall tales and poignant recalls were interspersed with cold beer and fried chicken. Hugs abounded. As a departing gift the nurses and clerks and therapists had spent months creating a memory quilt. Each unique block was an individual token of love and fond memories. There were many other gifts as well--- handmade with loving care or purchased with my interests in mind.

I was deeply moved by a framed poem written by one of our nurses. It was a child's prayer of thanks for the gift of life as a tribute to my special healing touch. I had always felt blessed with an intuitive understanding of the many problems facing the tiny wards placed in my care. More than eight thousand of them had passed my way, fighting off death day by day. I possessed a sixth sense, if you want to call it that, of just what intervention needed to be done to improve the status of my delicate charges. This talent was a gift from God and sometimes amazed even me. I tried never to take it for granted that miracles were being performed through my skills but not by my power.

Some of my former patients and their parents and siblings were at the picnic. Many of them remembered well: the tiny infant covered with wires and tubes; the family enduring days of despair and sleepless nights while their newborn struggled for survival and eventual autonomy; the joyous day of discharge when the baby was at last assimilated into the nurturing environment of home.

In the still heat of the city that glorious summer afternoon I surveyed my domain, as it were, and paused again to consider the decision I had made to leave the practice of medicine. Abandoning the training of a lifetime would leave an enormous void in my identity. The security of the hospital environment beckoned me to continue my work in its haven of familiarity with these dedicated co-workers whom I loved.

Friends and peers questioned my decision to retire at the peak of my career--the pinnacle of my success-- as they were quick to point out. It was difficult to convince my medical family that it was precisely at this point that I wanted to leave; to go out on top. At age forty-nine I ostensibly had many productive years ahead of me.

On the other hand, my very soul cried out for a different life style. I was simply tired beyond explanation. I wanted time for myself and time for my daughters. We deserved to experience life that was not shared with pagers, telephones and families in need. It would be a relief to attend dance recitals and school programs that were not interrupted by some crisis that usurped my family's togetherness. Jessica and Hiliary had tolerated our quixotic existence with grace and aplomb far beyond their years. Countless times the demands of my job had altered or obliterated plans they had made. We had all been inconvenienced beyond numeration: meals on the fly; clothes grabbed still-damp from the dryer; friends stranded or abandoned at school, at church, at restaurants. The odd behavior of the

Watkins household was tolerated by those people whom our lives touched because they understood our dedication to a cause greater than that of domestic tranquility.

Before the girls were old enough to stay at home alone, they had to accompany me to the hospital for emergencies. While I attended to the immediate crisis the nursery staff would entertain Jessica and Hiliary. During day shift they would be given toys and snacks and wheeled around the NICU on a supply cart. In the middle of the night they would be carried up the back stairwell and put into bunk beds in the physician's on-call room.

Fortunately my children adapted rapidly to abrupt changes. They felt right at home watching television with obstetricians and anesthesiologists. The medical staff members were always gracious and tolerant. When the acuity of the NICU emergency abated sufficiently for me to leave the unit, I would collect the girls and all their paraphernalia. Whenever possible we would continue whatever activity we had been engaged in before the current interruption.

I was solidly anchored to my retirement plans. My partners, however, weren't so sure about the wisdom of my decision. I thought they were going to miss me a lot more than they admitted! After all, a female associate's presence in the office and in the unit helped keep the men in line, to my way of thinking. I smoothed out their rough masculine edges.

Stewart Lawrence was the most recent addition to our neonatology group. He and I had formed a close professional bond from long weeks of tandem duty. His laid-back attitude and grace under pressure belied the dexterity with which he solved problems. We complimented each other's abilities, and Stewart buffered my jackhammer approach to patient care.

Steven Mayfield had been at St. Luke's for five years, but he was, to me, the least familiar of my partners. I admired his impressive store of information. The speed and thoroughness with which he completed daily working duties was admirable. No problem was too complex for Steve to solve or too insignificant for him to investigate. His deftness in dealing with multiple simultaneous crises was legendary. His compassionate interaction with families was obvious in their subsequent devotion to him.

Of my three associates I would miss Matthew most of all. He had come to St. Luke's at my invitation ten years earlier when solo coverage of the unit threatened to overwhelm me. Together we had struggled diligently to make our NICU one of the best in the country. The introduction of clinical studies and research projects into our programs had brought us national recognition.

Matt's quiet intensity camouflaged a reckless and fun-loving spirit. This was a man who raced stock cars and thought sky diving was a cool way to spend a day off. We had a natural working compatibility that made it easy to switch our schedules and vacation days without complicated readjustments in patient care. We could interchange orders and surgical procedures and charting without a hitch. Continuity in staffing protocols and family counseling was assured by our identical professional standards. Yes; I would miss Matt's casual good looks, his wonderful smile and his mutual admiration.

After the picnic the last two days of my

professional career were anticlimactic. At four o'clock on Friday afternoon, June 29, I took the final tape from my dictation-phone and turned off my pager for the last time. A feeling of finality settled over my spirit as I walked down the hall to my office.

With tears in her eyes, my secretary handed me my last official message: "GOODBYE DR. WATKINS. WE LOVE YOU AND WE'LL MISS YOU. YOU HAVE BECOME A LEGEND IN YOUR OWN TIME!" Signed: staff of the NICU.

CHAPTER 2
THE COLONEL

Michael Robbins carefully completed a pre-flight walk-around of his plane, checking the tires, fuselage, and weapons mountings. He stretched stiffly and ascended the ladder into the open cockpit of the forward pilot's seat. The fighter jet gleamed in the early morning sun. He loved its sleek lines and sky-gray color. His unadorned olive flight suit was a perfect counterpoint to the precisioned orderliness of the instrument panels as he closed the canopy and began inspection of switches and levers. He systematically reviewed the high-tech systems: HEADS UP display, RADAR, INFARED etc. until he was satisfied that all were good-to-go. The officer sat in the cockpit methodically running through his pre-flight checklist. Following the same procedure as he had done a thousand times before, the colonel tried not to let routine lull him into complacency. If he slipped into a pattern of confirmation by rote memory, he could overlook a miscue in one of the dozens of gauges around and below him. At the supersonic speeds of the airplane, the margin of error for the pilot was exceedingly slim. A minor miscalculation could send the jet into a fatal dive, augering it into the ground at MACH ONE.

When the checklist was completed Colonel Robbins inspected the remainder of his flight gear--G-suit, life vest, helmet, oxygen mask--and strapped himself into the seat. His long slender frame sank into place as if on a familiar sofa. He opened up radio communications with the control tower for the Duluth International Airport. The throbbing of the giant Pratt-and-Whitney F100 engines was a reassuring and soothing sound to a seasoned fighter pilot. Mike felt a fondness for the airplane much as he imagined a NASCAR driver must feel for his favorite racing car.

After receiving clearance for departure, Mike taxied across to his assigned runway. The F-16 pulsed into place on the vast straightaway, hesitated a moment, then shot down the tarmac like a demented metal mosquito. It cleared the end lights of the airport effortlessly and streaked off across Lake Superior with rapidly increasing speed and altitude.

Soaring through the clear skies above Minnesota, pilot and machine were briefly released from the constraints of civilization and the laws of gravity. The officer reveled in the power and performance of his aircraft as the unfettered duo frolicked in the air. Cocooned in his chariot of steel, Mike felt an exhilarating sense of freedom. Flying was his life; his love; his purpose.

After he returned from the training mission and had

tucked in his baby for the day, Colonel Robbins headed for the locker room. He found it relaxing to be back in Minnesota even though he was only a visiting instructor now. A quick shower and a very late breakfast and he could be in the commander's office by noon.

CHAPTER 3

ON THE ROAD

H is eyes were narrowed to slits in his lean face and tears oozed from their corners as witnesses to the bite of the cold wind. He held his head over the side of the pickup bed and let his tongue loll out of his mouth as far as it would go. This was Sam's favorite place. Traveling was his favorite pastime. It mattered not the occasion nor the distance. Weather conditions were irrelevant. As soon as the tailgate dropped, the dog propelled himself into the back of the truck and assumed his position. Even a one-mile trip to the convenience store would elicit a rapturous response from this simple creature.

Sam was of very mixed heritage---the result of generations of apparently random procreation. He appeared to be an unsightly mixture of yellow Labrador retriever and pit bull. When he was dropped off on our doorstep by friends of the children, Sam quickly won our hearts with his eagerness to please and his overweening enthusiasm for adventure.

The dog and I were motoring along state Highway 21. I was toasty in the cab of my '89 Ford and Sam was cold but happy in the rear. We were heading north on a wintry afternoon in mid-April in the high mountains of central Idaho. A country music ballad wailed from the radio. My off-key voice provided a dissonant counterpoint to the mournful tune. It was a good thing ole Sam was riding outside. My singing made him whine. It had that effect on my family also. Sam might not have been of noble birth but he did discriminate between the qualities of some things.

The late afternoon sky was cloudless. The crystalline brilliance seemed frozen to the backdrop of the forest. Snow lingered on branches of lodgepole and ponderosa pines. It outlined the log-worm fences that bordered the highway and meandered across open spaces that would metamorphose into meadows of wild flowers in a few weeks.

The snowplow had passed earlier in the day and left irregular drifts along the right-of-way. Tops of road signs and shoulder markers could be seen protruding through the mounds like skeletal digits. Creeks were swollen with early spring runoff. Forest debris clogged many of them, producing transient waterfalls and eddies. No deer or elk were visible but I knew they were just inside the tree line waiting patiently for twilight. Game animals grew large in the Stanley basin. They gathered in small herds at the edges of pastures along Valley Creek where the grass beneath the snow was more accessible.

Sam was riding on his dog throne---a lopsided cardboard box containing books, off-season clothing and other leftovers. The truck was piled high with camping gear, skis, kitchen utensils and an odd dresser or two. Most of the items were functional and represented the remains of fifteen years of homesteading in Boise. My younger daughter, Hiliary, had her own apartment now and was the recipient of much of the furniture and better appliances. Her older sister, Jessica, had little space in her dormitory room at Boise State University and made do with a paucity of personal accoutrements.

The girls and I had recently moved out of our home, which was now lost in the uncaring wasteland of the real estate market. The Watkins women were rearranging their physical and psychological lifestyles. As the girls moved slowly into adulthood I planned to become a hermit in the hills. What implements seemed essential for the greenhorn style of ranching I had in mind were dumped haphazardly on top of the great stumps of black locust trees protruding over the rails of the utility trailer that was wobbling merrily along behind the old brown truck. I felt a euphoric sense of freedom.

It was now almost two years since my retirement and nearing spring of 1997. I had not been resting on my laurels. In fact, I had hardly been resting at all. In my customary impulsive fashion I had immediately rushed off from St. Luke's to pursue a life-long ambition to be a teacher. Perhaps it was my aborted college dream to become a chemistry wizard that led me to at last officially scratch my professorial itch.

Boise State University had an enrollment of 15,000

students. Its Schools of Engineering and Nursing were outstanding. Its bright orange-and-blue school colors on the Bronco mascot were outlandish. I had stepped onto this campus as guest faculty in August of 1995. I was there to teach Health Sciences 201—a physiology class designed primarily for sophomore students in the respiratory therapy program. I pursued my passion for teaching with great vigor. The youthful energy of my students was stimulating while their lack of comprehension of the difficult subject matter was sometimes appalling.

In leading the students through the intricate workings of the human heart and lungs and kidneys, I had found my niche. It gave me great joy to see them grasp a concept, to watch understanding click into place in their minds as I labored to explain complicated cellular reactions and membrane potentials. As the semester progressed assorted bits of information fell into place in their heads like puzzle pieces.

As for myself, happily buried knee-deep in my students' research papers and examination results, I was in my element.

When the second term began in January, I switched gears to medicine again and embarked upon HS 304. This class was limited to third-year respiratory therapy students learning the delicate art of dealing with sick children. Teaching them how to cope with the babies in the NICU was my job. They were terrified of their tiny charges. I tried to give the students a core of basic skills upon which they could build sound clinical judgments and instill in them the ability to handle their fragile patients with thoroughness softened by compassion.

The Sawtooth Mountains came into view as Sam

and I roared down the hill past the scenic overlook on Highway 21. As always, the first sight of them filled me with happiness and an intense feeling of coming home. Their jagged peaks stood out in bold relief against the clear sky like rows of teeth on a saw made of gray granite for Vulcan. Even in April the mountains still wore thick caps of snow. In the thin air they appeared freshly spray-painted---gun-metal gray topped with white enamel. In immutable splendor, the perfection of their beauty made my heart ache.

The grandeur of this region prompted Congress to create the Sawtooth National Recreational Area (SNRA) in 1972. It encompassed 756,000 acres of incomparable beauty and the Sawtooth Wilderness Area was smack dab in the middle. It was this rugged land of serrated peaks, pristine lakes, and alpine meadows against which our little piece of heaven abutted.

The Stanley basin stretched along the northern edge of the Sawtooths. As Sam and I dropped rapidly from the overlook, subtle signs of spring were evident. Even the smallest rivulets had been turned into tiny rivers by the melting snow. The southern exposure of hillsides and roof tops showed deep concavities where the sun had warmed layers of snow, causing them to collapse upon themselves.

I switched music to the soundtrack from the movie "The Man from Snowy River" and cranked up the volume to headache level. My spirit soared in unison with Bruce Rowland's magnificent score as we rolled into the town limits of Stanley: population 69.

WELCOME TO STANLEY. GATEWAY TO THE SAWTOOTH WILDERNESS. An old wooden sign on the outskirts of town made this proclamation. It had been placed there by our friends, Selma Lamb and Sheldon Hentschke, who operated a realty office from their home just beyond this weathered sign. As the dog and I passed by, admiring Sheldon's ever-expanding collection of yard art, there was no hint of the disaster that would virtually land me in their doorway in three days' time.

Beyond the Hentschke's, at the abrupt end of Highway 21, the town of Stanley was nestled against the foothills at the east end of the basin. Here the merrily meandering Valley Creek joined the Salmon River which headed northeast parallel to state highway 75. A small mesa arose from the town center and provided a grass landing strip for the airport. A city park with a panoramic view of the Sawtooths flanked the schoolhouse, where one teacher and one aide guided thirty students across grades one through eight.

High school children commuted sixty miles down river to the Custer county seat of Challis. It was a daunting trip, especially in inclement weather, and most teenagers made other living arrangements for the school term. Religious services held in the non-denominational chapel could not help but be inspired by the undeniable evidence of divine creation visible through every window. A small Baptist church on the outskirts of town held Sunday services year-round as well as campfire ministry and mid-week bible study.

Stanley town proper consisted of 308 acres surrounded by the majesty of the SNRA. Permits for residential and business construction were closely regulated by the city council to maintain a pioneer appearance. Rustic buildings and unpaved streets continued the mining-town atmosphere. Ace of

Diamonds was the main street, all two blocks of it, and accommodated the post office, artisan's guild, a small hotel, and seasonal gift shops and eateries. Two saloons offered period-piece ambience, complete with pot-bellied stoves where one could thaw out on minus-thirty-degree evenings. There were no sidewalks.

The Mountain Village complex was owned by the late Bill Harrah's StanHarrah Corporation and served the locals as well as the tourists. The motel was constructed of lodgepole pines and had simple but attractive rooms. Meals were served at convenient hours in the adjoining restaurant. The bar did a booming business on weekends when ranch hands and cattlemen mingled with the visitors. The mercantile carried on in the grand old tradition of the country store. After choosing a cut of meat from the cooling bin, one might browse through the book racks and the hardware section and finish up with a video rental, a bottle of wine and a latte.

The permanent population of Stanley peaked at ninety-nine in the mid-eighties, but a slow attrition thinned its ranks. Over the years the economy of the Stanley basin shifted from livestock, timber, and mining to recreation and tourism. There were over a million visitor days in the SNRA in 1996 and supportive services were provided by the town. There were cabins to accommodate river rafters and kayakers and two clothing stores specializing in outdoor wear and gear. Many businesses were dormant from November until May but there seemed to be a gradual movement toward winter sports that owners hoped would provide a stimulus for year-round operation.

At 6,200 feet elevation, the Stanley basin received an

average annual precipitation of sixty inches, mostly as snowfall. The summers were short and enchanting, with temperatures around eighty degrees and skies as blue as lapis lazuli. The winters were harsh, with long stretches of sub-zero days made more bearable by bright sunshine and low humidity. Stanley frequently registered with the weather service as the coldest spot in the nation. The natives used humor to deal with the weather and highway closures due to blizzards and avalanches.

It was now later and colder than I had anticipated. I rolled down the window and let in the clear cold mountain air as Sam and I drove the remaining eight miles south of town along the Sawtooth Valley in the twilight. When we pulled to a stop before our gate it was obvious that the dog and I would have to walk the final hundred yards to the cabin. The snowplow had piled up an impressive barricade across the driveway, which was buried under three feet of snow. Since both the temperature and the sun were dropping rapidly, I turned the truck in the road, backed into the snow as far as I dared, and unhitched the trailer.

I laced on snowshoes and stepped awkwardly over the gate. Sam hesitated a moment, then catapulted out of the truck and promptly disappeared into a drift. He dug his way to the surface and raced off through the snow, leaving large uneven holes in the landscape. To say he cavorted would be implying a humanly response, but he did seem overjoyed. Perhaps he was simply relieved to finally be out of the truck.

I was panting long before I got to the cabin and my legs trembled with the effort of forging through the heavy snow. The thermometer on the front porch revealed a temperature of nineteen degrees. When I opened the front door of the cabin the frigid stale air seemed to me to be the aroma of paradise.

It would be an overstatement to say that our house claimed to have a décor but its eclectic mix of leftovers had a certain charm. The main room was covered with an ancient, unattractive, orange shag carpet. Sam and I did not hesitate to march in dropping large globs of melting snow on the floor.

My first order of business was to start a fire. A large Timberline stove stood in the middle of the room and consumed unbelievable amounts of firewood. It soon gave off comforting warmth and congenial crackles. When I had closed the cabin the previous October, I had left the wood box full of fuel. I was grateful now for that foresight. Digging firewood out of the snow in the cold darkness would simply have been beyond my capabilities at that moment.

A bowl of stale cereal sufficed for my dinner. I had a backpack full of bottled water and dog food but few provisions for myself. This night I would go to bed hungry but Sam had Evian and Gravy Train.

CHAPTER 4
JET JOCKEY

M ike Robbins had enlisted in the United States Air Force in 1971 fresh out of high school. He received training as an air traffic controller at Kincheloe AFB in Sault Ste. Marie, Michigan. At the end of the Vietnam War he entered the Minnesota Air National Guard (ANG) and was commissioned as a lieutenant in 1975. He flew in the RF-4 as the navigator or Weapons Systems Operator (WSO) or "Wizzo". The F-4 was to remain his personal favorite aircraft although he was experienced in flying a variety of other fighter jets.

In the Phantom, the back-seater, the Wizzo, also had a control stick, and Robbins often flew the plane during part of the training exercises. He had a natural talent for piloting and followed through on this promise by completing pilot training at Laughlin AFB in Del Rio,

Texas in 1981. He had found his calling and his passion.

Robbins' preferred combat training sortie was a high-speed, low-altitude reconnaissance mission. He got a thrill out of skimming along valley floors and rocketing over the surfaces of the Great Lakes at the speed of sound. He considered himself a hard-working average pilot with above-average leadership skills. He parlayed these skills and work ethic in the Minnesota Air National Guard into a series of promotions and became a squadron commander in 1991. At this time his unit began flying the F-16 as its primary aircraft.

Mike likened flying the Viper to sitting on top of a needle traveling at 500 knots per hour. The plane's powerful engines and streamlined body and sophisticated weapons crouched below the cockpit. The glass-surrounded canopy allowed the pilot and his trainee (when present) to have an unrestricted view of their airspace. When the planes flew in the typical combat unit, called a two-ship formation, the pilot was able to keep close watch over his wingman's "six"---the airspace directly behind his flying partner.

Despite paperwork and desk assignments, the jet jockey was able to get plenty of "stick time", i.e. actual flying experience. The pure joy of cruising at 30,000 feet made all the mundane earth-bound parts of his job tolerable. Occasionally Mike and other instructor/trainee pairs engaged in a simulated high-altitude, high-speed, multi-aircraft battle---a dogfight called a furball.

In his spare time Mike liked to fish. He had two teenagers who shared his love of the outdoors. The three of them went on outings and traveled together when time permitted. He was happy in Minnesota and content with his military career. A mandatory twenty-year retirement time was rapidly approaching, however, and the lieutenant colonel was not yet ready to hang up his ANG wings. Early in 1996 an opportunity to extend his service time to thirty years and to continue as both commander and flying instructor presented itself.

Robbins was appointed Director of Operations for the Washington Air National Guard, headquartered at McChord AFB in Tacoma. He left Minnesota with some reluctance but looked forward to an exciting chapter in his career.

Mike eagerly anticipated all the fishing adventures awaiting him in a new life near the ocean. He bought a comfortable condominium overlooking the waters of south Puget Sound in the small village of Gig Harbor. The civilian portion of the jet jockey settled into a busy and rewarding routine. He bought a new Isuzu sports utility vehicle and exercise equipment and running shoes. Life was lovely for almost a year.

The jet pilot was doing what he loved most---flying. He received a promotion to full colonel in March of 1997. He had a nice home in a beautiful location and enough free time to take advantage of almost unlimited opportunities for outdoor activities. What the commander did not know was that a darkness loomed on the horizon that he could never have anticipated.

CHAPTER 5

HOMESTEAD

Two miles from our cabin in the Sawtooth Valley was the community of Obsidian. This small cluster of buildings was once an important link between the settlements of Stanley and Sawtooth City. Miners and ranchers traversed the long narrow valley en route to trading centers in Challis and Ketchum. The fifty-mile round trip between the north and south ends of the valley might take two days or longer.

Snowshoes or skis were the prevailing mode of transportation in the deep snow. In wintertime homes along the rudimentary road provided impromptu stopovers for travelers marooned by inclement weather. When a seasonal storm blew in, one's unexpected house guest might be forced to remain for several days. Settlers kept extra food and bedding available for such minor inconveniences. Drop-ins were always welcomed. Folk passing through the valley brought news and gossip and helped alleviate the boredom of a long winter.

Obsidian was once a bustling community with numerous dwellings and businesses. It boasted an air strip, still visible from the foothills, and some really unattractive mobile-home and trailer parks. When the SNRA was established, scenic easements were purchased by the federal government to ensure the continuation of the aesthetic appeal of the area. Most of the buildings in Obsidian were demolished or sold and moved to other sites.

A post office was established in Obsidian in 1918 and continued to function, with a few interruptions, until 1947. Mr. Harry Fleming, about whom you will hear more, played an integral role in this vital service. Dressed in wool trousers and a battered sheepskin coat, warmed by flannel long-johns and a fur hat, Harry was a familiar sight in the communities as he carried the mail from Stanley to Obsidian six days a week. Later his route would be extended to Ketchum and he would make this often-hazardous journey until his retirement in 1975. In the bitter cold of deep winter Harry would be often be greeted by the postal patrons with a hot cup of cider and the sinew-thawing heat of a roaring fire. Perhaps a nip of spirits would be added to the cider to ensure that he warmed up quickly.

Mr. Harry Pearce came into the Sawtooth Valley in 1928. He brought his family and all their possessions in two covered wagons. Coming west from Idaho Falls along the Lemhi Valley and the Salmon River canyon, the Pearce family hoped to make a new life for itself in this remote and somewhat inhospitable place.

Of the one-hundred-and-sixty acres allotted for

homesteading, Mr. Pearce selected the most usable eighty acres along the river for his home site. The ground was porous and full of rocks. It grew many deer willows and little grass. Mr. Harry didn't mind, for ranching and farming were not in his game plan. The flat ground and limitless water supply from the Salmon River suited his needs for sawmilling just fine.

For two decades Mr. Pearce produced lumber and posts and his unique style of homemade pine furniture. The saplings used for the tables and chairs still had their bark on, but they were durable and inexpensive. His children, Martine and Raymond, grew up in the rugged simplicity of the homestead. They thrived in the harsh winters and lovely summers. The children made the most of limited opportunities for formal schooling. The unstructured school of the great outdoors taught them the fundamentals of survival. The absolute need for neighborly interaction taught them the fine art of friendship.

Mr. Ed Fleming operated a sawmill in Ketchum, Idaho, until 1922. With his teams of oxen and mules, Ed brought lumber and mining equipment over the White Cloud Mountains into the Sawtooth Valley. His sons, Fred and Harry, made many trips via Galena Pass with their father and grew to love the beautiful country and its hardy inhabitants. Harry moved to the valley in 1930 and three years later married Mr. Pearce's sixteen-year-old daughter, Martine.

The newlyweds received the south forty acres of the Pearce homestead as a wedding gift and built a small cabin there. The Flemings called their little ranch "the Poor Farm." Such designation was arguable as the soil proved too shallow and sandy to do more than support a few cows and sheep. The short growing season excluded most crops and limited the variety of garden produce. Family income was primarily due to Harry's job as mail carrier and to Martine's prized hand-sewn quilts.

In 1950 the Fleming's simple log home burned to the ground, taking with it most of their possessions. With the help of neighbors and Stanley folk, the Flemings were quickly able to purchase a replacement house. They obtained an old government Civilian Conservation Corps barracks building from the deserted Cobalt mining community and moved it onto the property. As finances permitted they added indoor plumbing and a bathroom. Martine and Harry raised four children in love and simplicity in the small dwelling. This remodeled rectangle, with its bright yellow enamel cabinets and sagging ceilings, became our home in 1994.

We euphemistically called our place the JJ Ranch. It was not technically a ranch since there was not a head of livestock in sight. The rusting barbed wire fence rambled restlessly around the perimeter, falling down here and there. Elk crossed the river and grazed in the back wetland bringing much of the fence along with them, considering it merely a nuisance.

Much of the land that Mr. Fleming struggled to convert to pasture reverted to its native flora of sagebrush and deer willows once it was neglected. Scattered about in random piles was an abundance of scrap iron in the form of antiquated farm machinery. There were also decomposing heaps of bed frames, washing machines, wagon and automobile parts; all slowly returning to nature. Some of these ranching relics were partially buried and overgrown with bushes. Some lay abandoned in a haphazard row of rusting rubble along the terrace line above the fish pond.

The barn was our pride and joy. Built in the early forties, it had aged gracefully even though it stood a bit askew. The western side was a rich copper color, burnished by decades of unfiltered sunlight. The ground had settled over the years, leaving the building listing to the east about five degrees from the vertical, lending to the barn a certain air of nostalgia.

The decor of our 800-square-foot cabin was late twentieth-century flea market. The carpets varied wildly in texture and hue, having been purchased at remnant sales room-by-room whenever the spirit moved the owners. The kitchen was built along one side of the main room almost as an afterthought. The canary yellow enamel of the cabinets and doors was somewhat overwhelming. Rather than struggle to overcome this decorative mishap, we accentuated it with an equally gaudy sunflower motif that somehow blended right in.

An aged orange/green/brown shag carpet spread over the large main room like a lunar landscape. It continued to show the wear associated with muddy boots and large wet dogs. Caulking around the old multi-pane single-glass windows had disintegrated, rendering them useless for insulation. This defect raised an issue in January when the temperature plunged to minus forty degrees and snow sifted through the holes to pile up on the inside window ledges. I guess the Flemings coped with this problem by wearing thermal underwear and sleeping under lots of Martine's beautiful quilts.

Our nearest neighbors were Craig and Betty

Rember, who purchased the old Pearce homestead in 1953 and settled there permanently in 1976. They offered pithy advice on how to correct our ranching misadventures and entertained us with tales of their colorful past. The Rember's annual Fourth of July pancake breakfast was one of the highlights of the summer. It served as a perfect example of the family's legendary hospitality. Hordes of folk came from the Stanley basin and the Sawtooth Valley to enjoy the good food and fellowship. Sheldon always arrived to wield a spatula wearing his trademark Uncle Sam knickers and blouse, complete with red-white-and-blue-striped pith helmet.

Sam and I watched the lights go out at the Rember's house as we huddled before the fire in our own little cabin on our own little homestead. When we settled into our respective beds, tired and content, I was without a clue as to the calamity that would descend upon me the following day.

CHAPTER 6

A PILOT GOES DOWN

Two weeks after his return to Tacoma from the training mission in Minnesota, Colonel Robbins signed up for his annual physical examination at Camp Murray, located just across Interstate 5 from McChord Air Force Base and Fort Lewis. The commander was in excellent health. He had no concerns about passing his medical evaluation with "flying" colors. He jogged and lifted weights and maintained a streamlined silhouette. He had never been a smoker and drank limited amounts of wine and cocktails.

A standard battery of tests was required yearly by the Washington Air National Guard. The officer had other commitments vying for his attention. He wanted to get the examination completed early in the week. The muscles in the back of his neck were always tight. This symptom was a common finding among fighter pilots and Mike was accustomed to the minor discomfort. After a dinner of pasta and salad, he dutifully climbed on the treadmill in his condo and began his standard ninety-minute workout.

The pilot struggled a bit more than usual through his routine. Sweating profusely through the completion of his sit-ups exercise, Mike was seized by an incredible pain in the back of his head. It was so abrupt and severe that he fell back on the floor, gasping more from the intensity of the pain than from exertion. He felt as though someone had slammed a hammer into the base of his skull.

Mike slowly looked around the room as his vision blurred. A wave of intense nausea washed over him, leaving Mike pale and shaking in its wake. He was alone in a room whose floor was undulating; whose walls and ceiling were ebbing and flowing; whose periphery was illuminated by weird flashes of yellow light.

The colonel cradled his head in his hands as he sat up slowly and prayed for the room to stop spinning. He rocked back-and-forth, moaning, and waited for the pain to subside. Rising cautiously, Mike crept into the bedroom and lay down on the bed. With his eyes closed to block out the wavering walls, he willed his body to relax. Here a twitch and there a jerk revealed muscle groups protesting the unexpected abrupt halt to their strenuous labors.

"What in the hell just happened?" Mike wondered aloud in misery and confusion. The dark burning pain in his head baffled him. The pilot assumed that he had seriously strained some muscles in his already stiff neck. His sweat-drenched clothing soon became clammy in the cool night air. Mike pulled the bedspread over himself although his chills were more related to shock than to temperature. He hoped that by morning the bizarre episode would seem like only a bad dream. Still moaning from the pain in the back of his head, the jet pilot at last fell into a troubled sleep.

CHAPTER 7
CATCHING A GLIMPSE

Friday the eighteenth of April dawned cold and bright. I, for one, was not awake to watch the sun rise over the foothills. It was midmorning when I crawled out of my warm blankets to rekindle the fire. Sam had snored and moaned all night beside the bed. He hesitated when I opened the front door and booted him out into the chilly air.

Breakfast was another gastronomical futility. Sam and I needed food. I planned to head for the Mercantile later in the day and have an entire blackberry cobbler with ice cream for dinner.

I picked up the telephone and was greeted by absolute silence. Dead as a doorknob. Swell! There was a pay phone at the convenience store in Obsidian. I would call the phone company from there and also give Robert a ring. My husband usually kept his worries to himself but

I knew that he would fret and gnaw at the edges of his concern until he heard from me. As events would transpire, my telephone disconnection would very shortly become an issue with dire consequences.

A few items of rejected apparel still hung in the closet from seasons past. I dressed in mismatched layers of clothing and went outside to do chores. Glancing at the thermometer as I skated across the ice on the front porch, I noted that the nighttime single-digit temperature had risen to nineteen degrees again. In the brilliant sunlight the day seemed much warmer as I strapped on my snowshoes and headed for the creek in the back pasture.

My first task was to collect water from the spring. Our water was marvelous—clear and cold—pure but not tasteless. One bucket for flushing the commode and one for drinking and dishes should do Sam and me for the day. Later I would get around to the plumbing. It would take me an hour at least to go into the frosty basement and prime the pump and flush all the antifreeze from the pipes. If I had had an inkling of what was to come I would have hauled in gallons of water.

After packing down a path across the yard with my snowshoes, I clomped out to the truck in a wide-based waddle. The morning crust on the snow collapsed into its softer inner layers with each laborious step. This unloading process was going to be more difficult than I had reckoned. I considered myself to be in good physical condition but the exertion of transporting supplies left me gasping and sweating.

On the third trip from the truck to the house I slogged along with a heavy night stand. About fifty feet from the front porch I put down my load and straightened up to take a few deep breaths. From out of nowhere I was broadsided by a blow to the base of my skull as if I had been struck with a sledgehammer. I dropped to my knees in the snow like a stone.

My first horrified thought was that I had been shot in the head. Not that this idea made much sense. Had a meteorite dropped out of the clear sky and landed on me? Had a phantom assailant sneaked up behind me unaware? I knelt dumbfounded, unable to comprehend what had just happened to me.

An unpleasant burning sensation moved rapidly from my left fingertips to my right hand, crossing my shoulders and causing both arms to rise in the air of their own accord. The hairs of my skin prickled and stood on end.

I watched in detached amazement as my right arm began rhythmic jerking which I recognized as a seizure. These spasmodic muscle contractions lasted about thirty seconds and were accompanied by a generalized burning sensation that I could best equate with electrocution. Then an indescribable pain erupted in my head. I pitched forward in the snow and vomited and passed into blackness.

I don't know how much time elapsed. When I regained consciousness I was not aware of the cold--- only the surety that at any moment my skull was going to explode. I lay in a bank of slowly melting snow at the border of my own front yard dimly aware of the brutal realization that no one was coming to rescue me.

Basic instinct finally roused me from fatal inertia. Never mind that something awful was happening inside my brain. If I didn't get into the house right away I would succumb to hypothermia, thereby resolving all my obvious problems! Feeling as if someone was removing the top of my head with a dull saw, I crawled the endless distance to the doorway.

Brightly colored lights swirled before my eyes. The earth undulated. The row of lodgepole pines in the front yard swayed to-and-fro alarmingly. My snowshoes were a major hindrance but there was no way I could negotiate their removal. At last I slithered across the icy porch and pushed open the door. Sam darted in as I sprawled on the floor, crying and retching.

When the human body experiences a catastrophic insult, neurochemicals are released in massive quantities. They serve to propel the mind and body through the crisis at hand. A physiological collapse called *shock* often follows and I was in the throes of it now. My skin was clammy; my teeth chattered; my limbs rattled. Waves of nausea rolled over me, unrelieved by repeated vomiting. I lay prostrate in abject terror on the dismal shag carpet in a pool of yellow mucus. The pain in my head was unbearable.

Always in the truly awful gut-wrenching times of my life I have wanted my mother. My fear and pain bubbled to the surface in little whimpers. "Mother, help me!" "Mother, where are you?" Folded into a tight S-shape on the floor I prayed and wept and blew my nose on the sleeves of my jacket.

As the hours ticked by my prayers for deliverance mingled the spiritual and corporeal until pleas for my mother became cries to Heaven. God sent help in His own good time but not in the form of my mother.

He sent an angel.

Sam's cold nose on my cheek roused me a bit from

my misery. I still had an obligation to fulfill. I dragged my tortured body across the floor, snowshoes snagging on the carpet, and raked his food and water dishes off the cabinet and filled them. This small task renewed a cycle of vomiting and shivering and blackness.

After another block of lost time, I curled into a fetal position as close to the stove as possible. I noticed that steam was rising from my clothing but I felt chilled to the bone. Somewhere in time I inched into the bedroom and actually crawled into bed. As the electric blanket began to thaw my frigid body, my mind took another leave of absence.

The next forty-eight hours seemed to constitute a lifetime. The bright sunny days were incongruous with the bleakness of the personal drama being played out indoors. Had not the intense pain kept me grounded in reality I might have considered the situation a deranged daydream. I couldn't run away from the cold hard fact that something in my head had gone phlooey.

My single act of anything resembling heroism was my attention to Sam's welfare. He seemed to sense that my life was all akimbo and never moved far from my side. The mere presence of another living creature was a great comfort to me. I kept him supplied with water and food and managed to let him outside for calls of nature. To his good credit Sam maintained remarkable bladder control. Sometimes I would drift off and forget about the dog, only to struggle to the door hours later and find him shivering in the cold.

My own bodily needs were less easily met. I was too nauseated to hold down water so the few Tylenol I took to ameliorate my pain soon resurfaced. I prayed for unconsciousness as an escape from the agony in my head. At the same moment I was also terrified at the prospect that I might never wake up.

I must have slipped into some form of twilight because Friday became Saturday and I now had a second problem to deal with. When I tried to roll over in bed I could not move. Nothing in my body had gone mechanically amiss but a white-hot pain shot down my spine that made the intensity of the constant headache pale in comparison. Unable to deal with this dreadful new development, I simply cried myself into another period of oblivion.

A few hours later I awoke in a mental fog. An acute anxiety attack hovered on the edge of my sanity as I prayed earnestly for deliverance from my travails. A slight turn of my head sent a bolt of pain to my toe tips. Obviously my desperate situation had not improved. I lay there in despair, drowned in a sea of pathos.

Sammy's whine of discomfort brought me out of my morbid self-absorption. If I was destined to die from this mysterious malady I might as well go down in a blaze of action. After some awkward gyrations I tumbled off the side of the bed. Humping on all fours across my favorite shaggy terrain, I let a very grateful dog outside.

My foresight of stocking the wood box the previous autumn became part of my salvation. By rationing the supply of fuel I could keep the cabin marginally warm. I spent my time now lying on my side before the fire, back rigid as a poker.

At some point I became aware of the angel. There was no bright light or heavenly voice. But there was an unmistakable presence in the room. It seemed masculine in nature and hovered near my left shoulder.

I felt enveloped in serenity, and in that awesome comfort I lost all fear of dying. The angel remained nearby for long intervals, as real as the air around me. It often retreated into the edge of my awareness but never abandoned me.

During those terrible hours lying before the stove I began to catch a glimpse of the fine line between life and death. Never before had I seen that division so clearly nor dealt with it so intimately. In my profession, where the drive for survival was imprinted upon the smallest of infants, death often came suddenly. Now the possibility of my own demise was demanding immediate consideration. I became surprisingly at peace with the proximity of death, but when it did not come readily, I began to comprehend that my guardian angel had appeared to comfort me, not to escort me.

It is not in my nature to passively accept adverse circumstances. This catastrophic collapse of mine was no exception. Yes; I had been visited by a heavenly spirit. Yes; I felt a peaceful acceptance of my mortality. These truths did not imply, however, that I planned to capitulate to destiny without a fight. I continued my simple routine of caring for Sam and me as well as possible as Saturday faded into Sunday.

A new problem now faced the dog and me that had nothing to do with medical or spiritual matters. Our supplies of water and firewood were dwindling rapidly. I had no intention of dying from dehydration or hypothermia. Sam also deserved a finer fate than starvation. We did not have a plethora of options. Our best chance for obtaining assistance was driving into Stanley. This plan sounded like a reasonable solution for our tribulations but its implementation was not going to be an easy undertaking. The truck was a hundred yards away and I still couldn't get on my feet.

Dressing for the endurance crawl required minimal effort as I was still wearing Friday's outfit. My jacket was streaked with dried tears and nasal drips and vomit. All my clothing reeked with odors of wood smoke and old sweat. With a backbone screaming in protest and a head ready to burst, I secured the doors to the wood stove and closed the front door as Sam and I wiggled out into a cold overcast day. It was beginning to snow.

The dog made faster progress toward the truck than I did. The snow was crusted over and my knees and elbows kept popping through the crust as I made my way down the driveway on my belly. It took me almost an hour to crawl the 335 feet to the highway. Every ten yards I sprawled in the snow to let my head settle.

Crawling over the gate required a supreme effort and left me shaking from the strain. A fence post served as a prop for my becoming vertical; a lunge landed me at the truck door; a side mirror provided a grip to break my fall. The entire endeavor almost became shipwrecked when Sam, with great exhilaration, hurled himself over me into the front seat. Somehow he missed the fact that I was not hopping into the vehicle with my usual alacrity.

Battling waves of nausea and dizziness I finally got seated behind the steering wheel. There was actually some improvement in the head and spine departments once I was bent in the middle. Clinging to the wheel like a life preserver, I tried to focus on the task at hand. The keys were in their customary place in the cup holder. The heater blasted out cold air as I shakily drove onto Highway 75 and headed north. Fortunately there were few cars on the road that April Sunday at noon as the brown Ford wove its slow wobbly way toward Stanley.

My rejuvenated energy waned rapidly as Sam and I crept down the highway into town. Admitting that my condition was far beyond the aid of a telephone call, I slowly pulled into the Hentschke's driveway. I never stopped to think about what I would do if our friends were not at home. Obviously I was in no condition to mount a second attempt to rescue myself. I muttered an abbreviated but fervent prayer of thanks when I saw Sheldon reading a newspaper at the kitchen table. When Selma opened the door I fell into her arms.

CHAPTER 8
CRASH AND BURN

The jet jockey had no way of knowing that he had just experienced a sentinel bleed. Thirty per cent of aneurysm victims have a warning, or herald, hemorrhage. Their symptoms vary widely depending on the location and extent of the bleeding but a universal complaint is the unexpected, unexplained, abrupt onset of excruciating headache.

Almost all persons stricken with sentinel bleeds will have another episode of hemorrhaging within six weeks of the initial event. This second occurrence is often catastrophic and may be fatal within minutes. Like a quarter of the patients with ruptured aneurysms, the colonel was engaged in strenuous activity when his first bleed occurred. The temporary increase in blood pressure and heart rate that accompanies exertion multiplies the stress on the weakened arterial wall and may stretch it beyond its breaking point.

When he awoke on Wednesday morning Mike had a constant moderate headache and no appetite. During the rest of the week he stoically completed his annual flight physical with no other symptoms. The only abnormality discovered in the examination was his inability to read the eye chart. Mike had always had exceptional far vision. His evaluator attributed the change in visual acuity to Mike's age (44) and the stress of his directorship, and recommended glasses. The officer's repeated complaints of headache were also ascribed to stress as he consumed large quantities of Tylenol and aspirin in a vain attempt to find relief.

On Friday his medical evaluator at Camp Murray suggested that Mike should undergo a specialized brain scan, called an MRI (Magnetic Resonance Imaging), at Madigan Army Medical Center (MAMC) at Fort Lewis. He agreed to pursue the evaluation the following week and headed home, bedeviled by the relentless ache in his head.

"Stress," his examiner had said. Well; he had had the same level of stress for years and it had never produced a pain like this!

The late afternoon sun was directly in Mike's eyes as he drove across the Tacoma Narrows Bridge. The traffic had slowed to a crawl. On this lovely spring afternoon, May 2, the westbound lanes were crammed full of commuters returning to their homes on the Sound for a peaceful retreat from the frenetic activity in the city. There were also weekend escapees from Tacoma and Seattle bound for quieter and cooler destinations on the Olympic Peninsula. Perhaps they were planning camping trips in the national park or heading for Townsend at the tip of the peninsula for seafood and fishing.

"The Department of Transportation needs to do something about this ridiculous gridlock!" the pilot muttered to himself. Behind his aviator shades Mike was becoming annoyed both at the traffic and at his discomfort. He was tired after a long week and ready to get home to Gig Harbor. The pain in his head had shifted a bit and was now concentrated behind his left ear.

It took thirty minutes to creep off the bridge. The officer pulled into a shopping center already busy with the weekend crowds and parked his navy blue Trooper near the entrance to Albertsons Supermarket. "I'll run into the grocery store for some coffee," he thought. "It will be good to lounge around the house with a fresh cup of joe and watch ESPN. Time to see what plans Lou Pinella has for the Mariners this year."

Thankfully there was no line waiting in front of the coffee grinder. Mike chose a bag of Seattle's Best Breakfast Blend and dumped it into the bin. He selected fine grind to suit his Krups coffee maker and waited mindlessly for the machine to pulverize the beans.

Without warning the pilot became aware of an unpleasant tingling sensation throughout his body. He identified the feeling as electricity and instinctively looked down to see if he was standing in water. He was suddenly knocked off his feet by an explosion of pain in his head. Mike felt himself falling but could not make his arms move to break the fall. He saw the speckles in the off-white linoleum as the floor came up to meet him. His right collarbone cracked on impact but the colonel was unaware of the pain as his body jerked and twisted in a generalized convulsion.

When Mike regained consciousness he was lying on his back on a cool hard surface. Everything was black as pitch although he was certain that his eyes were open. "Am I in Heaven or Hell?" was his first coherent thought. He heard a female voice ask, "Mike, are you all right?" He felt someone touch his hand and was aware of a profound sense of disorientation. Dazed and confused the officer lay there in darkness, slowly absorbing the fact that he was indeed alive.

"Dear God! I can't see!"

Concerned supermarket customers and employees clustered around Mike as he lay sprawled in the aisle of the coffee/tea section wondering again with terrifying dismay what was happening to him. The Albertsons' manager recognized the officer's uniform and name tag and called MAMC for an ambulance. As he lay stunned on the floor in internal blackness awaiting medical attention, Mike became aware of the fact that his headache was gone.

CHAPTER 9

BOTH DOCTOR AND PATIENT

The Stanley Volunteer Ambulance Service on-call team members left their Sunday dinners to minister to my needs. Dick Stoney and Steve Lipus answered Selma's urgent call. They listened attentively to my story and symptoms. These earnest first responders did a brief examination to determine my stability and arranged for an ambulance transport to Wood River Medical Center in Hailey.

Sparkey Easom and his wife Mary Ellen were the emergency medical technicians (EMTs) who would travel with me. They were compassionate and skilled professionals. The team inserted an intravenous line into my arm, placed an oxygen mask on my face, and loaded me into the vehicle with little fanfare. It was snowing rather heavily by this time but our driver, Luanna Gunderson, had no intention of waiting for the snowplow to clear our route through the White Cloud Mountains.

The twisting journey over Galena Pass was accomplished slowly but safely due to Luanna's skillful driving. For me the ride was a torture. Due to the dreadful discomfort in my head and back I could not lie supine nor remain still. My ritual for dealing with pain had been perfected over the past three days. I pleaded with the Easoms not to strap me down and shortly thereafter dropped to my knees on the floor and vomited. I was too ill to care about the ignominy of my circumstance.

I began to cry as pain and misery overwhelmed me. Sparky put his arms around my shoulders and let me weep as I relinquished all control over my situation.

The ambulance arrived in Hailey rather expeditiously given the unfavorable road condition. The sun broke through the cloud cover as we pulled into the entrance of Wood River Hospital. I took this sign as a portent of better things to come. I was wrong.

We were met in the emergency ward by Dr. Jan Rosenquist, the physician on call for emergencies. She was very rapid and thorough in her examination and ordered a brain X-ray called a CAT (computerized axial tomography) scan.

The scanner looked like a horizontal beige cement mixer. It seemed menacing somehow, centered as it was in a small, cold, monochromatic room. I was immobilized on a wide board by straps across my knees and chest. Adhesive tape was stretched tightly across my forehead and lapped over the edges of my prison as if my head might go off on its own.

The board slid noiselessly into the mouth of the scanner until I was entombed in beige plastic. When the conveyor came to a halt, my eyeballs were level with a circular rim of lights. They began to rotate and hum in a surreal fashion.

"Beam me up, Scotty!" I thought, in nearly hysterical irrelevance.

The scanner unit turned 360 degrees and made serial x-rays of my cranial cavity like three dimensional slices in a loaf of bread. The procedure was painless and took about seven minutes. Nonetheless my latent claustrophobia made me exceedingly anxious. I hummed Christmas carols, swallowed a lot, hyperventilated a little, and tried not to panic.

Perhaps my diagnosis could be made and my fate sealed with the result of this one test. At the very least maybe I could finally have something stronger than Tylenol for my damn headache! The ambulance trip had intensified it to the intolerable point. I also had become aware of feeling an increasing fullness in my head rather as if someone had stuck a hose in my ear and turned on the faucet.

As we waited for the radiologist's interpretation of the CAT scan, the nurses kindly helped me to disrobe and take what my mother referred to as a "sponge bath." Soap and water and a toothbrush made a vast improvement in my social acceptability. The hospital gown did not cover much of my anatomy but it was definitely a step up from Friday's soiled attire.

Selma and her son, Joe Lamb, had followed the ambulance to Hailey. I was immensely grateful for Selma's comforting presence. She drove to the nearest market and bought a bottle of Sea Breeze to wash my hair. We chatted lightly about my predicament as she tried to keep my mood from plummeting.

"How can you joke about dying with clean teeth at

a time like this?" Selma asked with some dismay.

"What would you have me do? Wallow in self pity?" I returned rather testily.

While Selma was distracting my attention from the consideration of sinister possibilities, dear friend Sheldon was back in Stanley cleaning up the awful mess I had left in the cabin. He eventually returned my truck and Sam to Boise and left them with our former neighbors.

It was very alarming to observe the cardiac monitor during this time. My heart rate slowly dropped to forty-five, and my blood pressure was steadily increasing. Dr. Rosenquist was getting nervous as the condition known as increased intracranial pressure slowly compressed my brainstem against the base of my skull.

No wonder my head felt like a pressure gauge in use!

I lay on a narrow bed in the emergency room beneath the fluorescent glare of the procedure lamps watching my life force implode. I again caught a glimpse of the fine line. It seemed to me to be a rather simple move from life into death. Would I pass from one state into the other without being actively involved in the transition? Would I simply become a formless but cognizant entity in another dimension? Then again, I might just cease to be anything but a corpse. Amazed that I could contemplate mortality so dispassionately, I faded into a narcotic haze induced by a large dose of morphine.

Narcotics have potent analgesic properties. Following knee surgery and a dislocated shoulder morphine sulfate had become my drug of choice for pain control. For the first time in fifty-six interminable hours my headache was somewhat subdued. My spine no longer felt like my head was being unscrewed from my neck. I was able at last to rest without fidgeting even as my pulse and blood pressure continued in opposite and incorrect directions. Before this nightmare was over I would come to crave morphine and then ultimately to loathe it.

With several large sheets of developed x-rays in hand, Dr. Rosenquist walked in and dropped a bomb.

"You have a large subarachnoid hemorrhage and early hydrocephalus," she announced without fanfare.

To my trained ears this statement was particularly ominous even though not totally unexpected. My doctor held the x-ray films up to the overhead light. I could see the thin white line created by blood in the space between the middle and inner plastic-wrap-thin membranes, called meninges, surrounding my brain.

Blood is very irritating to the cells of the nervous system; hence my mother of all headaches and the burning intensity of a spine inflamed. The reaction was causing tissues to swell and thereby blocking the normal pathway for spinal fluid drainage. The four collecting chambers deep in my brain, called ventricles, were expanding with trapped fluid. This distention, or hydrocephalus, produced the feeling of fullness in my head and the dangerous trend in vital signs.

Dr. Rosenquist got down to really serious business.

"I think you may have a ruptured aneurysm," she stated flatly.

Aneurysm! Now there's a word to strike terror into one's heart. Not part of your everyday vocabulary, I'm sure. Perhaps it should be. In every mixed group of one hundred persons, two or three or four people will have some vascular anomaly that can be called by this name.

Some aneurysms occur on blood vessels elsewhere in the body but most of them exist in the fragile convoluted circulation of the central nervous system.

An aneurysm is a balloon-shaped bubble in the wall of an artery where it has been weakened. This frequently occurs at a junction where the vessel divides into smaller branches. These thinned spots may be caused by injury, aging, and hypertension. There is a slight predominance of females in the affected population, especially in women over the age of fifty. Most defects are congenital but not genetically linked to other immediate family members.

Aneurysms have an ugly habit of making themselves known by the sudden onset of excruciating headache followed rapidly by loss of consciousness, coma, and death. About thirty percent of aneurysmal disasters fall into this category. These unsuspecting victims collapse in front of their classrooms; die in their fishing boats; slump over their keyboards. Those who do not succumb immediately have a fifty-fifty chance of long-term survival.

An aneurysm patient must withstand a difficult operation to locate and close his defect, with the threat of death by exsanguination ever present. The stem portion of the leaky balloon is pinched together with clips made of non-ferromagnetic cobalt alloys. Once the defect is clipped, the patient is free of any risk of further hemorrhaging from that site.

If one escapes all the mishaps possible during surgery, the greatest concern in the days immediately post-operative is the specter of vasospasm. The combination of bleeding and surgical manipulation often causes arteries to constrict, thus limiting the amount of blood available to certain portions of the brain. This ischemia, in turn, may cause permanent damage to the brain tissue beyond the constriction. My family was soon to become very familiar with this menacing complication.

I tried to ignore the downhill march of the life signs constantly beeping on monitors near my bedside. The respite provided by the morphine allowed me to digest the fact that I was indeed headed for brain surgery—a prospect I found most distressing. We non-surgical doctors teasingly called our neurosurgical colleagues "head crackers" as a dubious term of endearment. We were occasionally guilty of making disparaging remarks about the caliber of their patients. Now I was about to become one of them.

As Selma and I waited for the helicopter that would transport me to St. Alphonsus Hospital in Boise, our conversation gradually dwindled as the full impact of Dr. Rosenquist's diagnosis settled on my shoulders like a lead cape.

When the stretcher was wheeled out to another ambulance for my ride to the airport in Hailey, the sun broke through the heavy clouds. A gentle breeze touched my face. A deep melancholy descended on me as I realized that I might have experienced the simple joys of sunshine and wind for the last time.

The ensuing one-hour helicopter flight was truly terrible. The transport stretcher was an ironing board in thin disguise. My back pain returned with a vengeance. The paramedics tried to ease my discomfort by letting me twist sideways under the straps and blankets. The EMTs cut a pair of headphones in half and taped one over whichever ear of mine happened to be exposed to reduce the noise of the engine.

The medic nearest me must have sensed how forlorn I felt for his hand never left me. A light touch on the shoulder or a pat on the foot let me know that he was ever vigilant. Since conversation was impossible over the noise in the chopper, he communicated his compassion by touch.

As I neared the limits of my tolerance the helicopter settled gently on the roof of St. Al's. The stretcher was lifted onto a gurney as the machine settled into the dust kicked up by its rotors. The worried face of my friend and colleague, who was now my personal physician, appeared above me.

"This is one hell of a note," growled Dr. Reedy.

I smiled in spite of my misery. "Hello, Peter. It's nice to see you, too."

He gave my hand a squeeze and said, "We'll take care of you. Don't worry."

Don't worry. Sure!

Dr. Peter Reedy. Friend and fellow intensivist. Not your archetypal neurosurgeon. Clad always in jeans and cowboy boots, Peter usually showed up for his esoteric work in a plaid shirt with the sleeves rolled up. I was certain there were no Armani suits in Dr. Reedy's closet. His straight dark hair was pulled into a ponytail hanging between his shoulders. I noticed streaks of gray and a receding hairline that had appeared since last we met. His eyes had their familiar twinkle but his face showed more concern than his gruff greeting suggested.

As we wheeled into some nonspecific place in the emergency ward Peter placed the CAT scan from Wood River Hospital on the fluorescent x-ray viewing box and stared at it intently. With a short knowing nod of his head he confirmed Dr. Rosenquist's impression. Without a word to me he picked up the phone and called the Radiology department and scheduled an immediate repeat scan to be followed by an arteriogram. Fortunately for me another dose of morphine took effect and I dozed off. I recalled climbing onto the scanner bed but slept through the second edition of radiological exploration.

I remained groggy until we hit the chill of the room set up for the arteriogram. It seemed an alien environment even though I had been in such rooms before with my own patients. I was cold and frightened and exhausted. Peter offered reassurance and brought me a blanket warmed in the heating closet. When I thanked him for his consideration, my neurosurgical friend explained dryly, "I'm not accustomed to having my patients complain of the cold. Most of them are comatose when they arrive in this room!"

The radiologist went about his duties with professional objectivity, occasionally muttering words of encouragement or instruction. Subdued murmuring of masked assistants in blue-gray scrub uniforms and skullcaps could be heard. Their paper booties rustled softly on the tiled floor as I took slow deep breaths and prepared myself for a very unpleasant experience.

An arteriogram is a procedure used to visualize the flow of blood into an organ or portion of the body. If there is an abnormality, the defect can be seen within the characteristic dark spider-web pattern of the circulation. A small plastic catheter is inserted into an artery proximal—nearer the heart—to the area of concern. Radiopaque dye is injected through the catheter into the bloodstream while x-rays are taken simultaneously. The fan-like network of dark blood vessels stands out in sharp contrast to the grainy grayness of the surrounding tissues.

In my case the catheter was about the size of # 2 pencil lead. The radiologist shaved my right groin and pubic area and scrubbed the skin with iodine-based antiseptic. After numbing the superficial muscles with a local anesthetic, he located my femoral artery by palpating its pulse. He skillfully inserted a larger plastic sheath, called a sleeve, into the vessel and threaded the smaller catheter through the sleeve into the artery. It passed through my pelvis and along my aorta---the huge artery just anterior to my spine.

When the catheter reached the takeoff of the left carotid artery going to my head, the doctor manipulated its tip well into the main stem of the vessel. He told me to breathe slowly and remain very still. As if I had any choice in the matter, since I was sedated and securely strapped to the bed! An automated syringe shoved a large pre-measured bolus of dye into my head as a rapid series of x-rays followed. The clacking of the machine reminded me of a camera shutter being repeatedly tripped. The staccato sound reverberated in the cold, gray, ceramic tile chamber.

The process was repeated on the right side of my head and then on the arteries at the base of my skull which supply blood to the cerebellum and brain stem. Early in the procedure I fell into a full-blown anxiety attack from being immobilized. Each injection of the dye produced an unpleasant generalized hot flash. Soon I was perspiring profusely and helplessly under the blanket. I cried silently and sweated through the remainder of the procedure.

Shortly after the arteriogram Peter reappeared at my bedside with Dr. Ron Jutzy, his associate. I was glad to see Ron, who was an old friend as well, but I took it as a bad sign that my case warranted a group discussion. This time I was right. The aneurysm was easily visible on the arteriogram as a clover-leaf-shaped balloon arising at a juncture of one of the arteries going to the left side of my cerebellum. I stared in morbid fascination at the aberration threatening my life while the rest of my composure fell apart.

The cerebellum crouches gingerly over the brainstem at the base of the skull. The complexity of the repair and the risks for complications mandated my referral to a facility whose medical staff had ample experience in handling both. Consensus was quickly gathered that I should be transported to Harborview Medical Center (HMC) in Seattle at once.

Dr. Reedy was soon on the phone to Robert, who was driving to Boise from Ft. Lewis. My husband was racing along Interstate 84, desperate to reach me. He was just west of Pendleton, Oregon when Peter handed the phone to me.

"How are you, Sweetie?" my husband asked with a crack in his voice.

My part of the conversation was very short. Robert agreed with Peter's referral and immediately headed back to Washington.

After a brief delay I was loaded into ambulance number three and taken to the Boise executive air terminal. This time the Life Flight transport team and I would be traveling in a small fixed-wing airplane. The Cessna was blessedly warmer and quieter than the helicopter had been as we set out on our two-hour flight. It was now nearing ten-o'clock on Sunday night, April 20th. I anxiously awaited my rendezvous with fate as we lifted off into the darkness.

CHAPTER 10
GROUNDED

A group of worried shoppers clustered around the slender man in a blue uniform who lay crumpled on the floor. Murmurs of concern rustled through the crowd as the Albertsons' staff maintained a wide circle of protection around their fallen customer.

Colonel Robbins was acutely aware of the actions of the Army medical technicians who arrived to care for him. They applied a brace around his neck as a precautionary measure, for he had already injured himself in the fall and subsequent seizure. Since his vision was impaired, Mike's other senses became sharply attuned to the stimuli of his environment. As he was loaded into the emergency vehicle for his short ride to MAMC, the colonel was bombarded by ordinary sounds: traffic noises from the street; the banging of car doors closing; the conversation of his attendants.

The warm spring air brushed over him lightly before the ambulance doors closed and engulfed him in a world of medical madness.

At Madigan the staff of the emergency room wasted no time in stripping the pilot of his apparel and personal items. Mike always wore a St. Michael's medal around his neck on a heavy silver chain. He was highly agitated about the possible loss of this precious amulet. His caretakers securely taped the medallion into his palm for safe keeping and good luck.

Their patient was wearing a neck brace so the Madigan medical attendants knew that his body should be minimally maneuvered. Therefore the emergency room nurses planned to cut the officer's uniform down the side seams and dismantle it in pieces. Mike pleaded with them to preserve his brown leather bomber jacket.

"If anything happens to me that jacket goes to my daughter!" he exclaimed. Perhaps Mike's concern for his material belongings seemed inappropriate to the medical staff under the circumstances of the patient before them, but for a man whose life had been regulated by strict order this loss of control pushed him unexpectedly near panic.

While his military personnel records at McChord AFB were being scanned for information and emergency notification telephone numbers, the officer underwent a rapid series of diagnostic tests, including a CAT scan of his head and neck. The eerie humming sound of the machine was intensified by the darkness pressing around him.

Mike intensely disliked being strapped down stem-to-stern with his head immobilized in a padded vise. When the scan revealed a large subarachnoid hemorrhage with blood in all four ventricles of his brain, Mike was immediately moved to the angiography room in Radiology for an arteriogram. The discomfort of the latter procedure was quickly forgotten as he lay in lonely darkness in the emergency ward wondering just what landmine inside his skull had detonated.

Short periods of oblivion followed; perhaps he was napping. He was in no pain and had repeatedly refused medication. True to his precise and orderly nature, what Mike really wanted was answers. Whatever his problem was, it could be isolated and remedied, and he wanted to get on with the fixing of it.

Drifting into consciousness once again, the pilot was aware that someone in the room was talking to a priest. He assumed that the man of cloth was there to administer last rites to the poor patient in the next bed. It wasn't until the priest touched his arm and spoke to him that Mike realized there *was* no roommate; the man of God was there to minister to *him*!

With alarm and fear and a degree of anger, Mike protested, "I am not going to die! I want to speak to a doctor!"

Dr. Anthony Bottini had been busy since the arrival of the jet jockey. After reviewing Colonel Robbins' CAT scan and arteriogram, the surgeon was gravely concerned. The officer had a large fusiform aneurysm on each vertebral artery just as it coursed from his neck into the base of his skull. The left defect was distorted with evidence of recent bleeding. As Assistant Chief of Neurosurgery at MAMC, Dr. Bottini was very familiar with the cataclysmic nature of aneurysms. Taking a deep breath, Dr. Bottini straightened his standard-issue narrow black medical corps tie and headed for the emergency room to talk with his patient.

Mike thought he was prepared to hear bad news but he was still taken aback when Dr. Bottini launched his grenade---the pilot had a ruptured blood vessel inside his head and it could bleed again at any moment. Another bleed would probably be fatal. Although the colonel was not yet fully aware of the fact, he was rapidly approaching the fine line between life and death. Mike's family had been notified of the seriousness of his situation but there was a very real possibility that he might not survive until his children arrived from Minnesota.

As Mike struggled to assimilate this information, his physician went on to inform him that surgical intervention was imperative. When the colonel asked about a second opinion, Dr. Bottini said, without hesitation, "You should go to Harborview Medical Center. The neurosurgeons there are the best in the northwest for repairing aneurysms."

This was Mike's first acquaintance with the term *aneurysm* but he would hear it many times in the months to come as its residue would forever linger in his life. In the still darkness of his despair the pilot could hear a helicopter warming up.

CHAPTER 11
ROOM WITH A VIEW

Skidding tires on wet tarmac jolted me from my semi-conscious state. I returned to awareness with great reluctance. The two-hour flight had been relatively peaceful after the torment of the helicopter ride. Perhaps a narcotic fugue improved my point of view but there was also relief in knowing what awaited me at Harborview. I was too physically depleted and mentally exhausted to deal with much contemplation.

Because of the fluid accumulating inside my head, my blood pressure continued climbing steadily. I could actually hear blood circulating through my brain. Each forward propulsion of blood from my strong slowing heart produced a psychic tidal wave with an audible crash as on a rocky shore. As I lay immobile in the steady hum of the aircraft, I could feel and see the blood pulsating through the retinal vessels in the backs of my eyeballs. This observation had its own morbid fascination and I had occupied myself for much of the journey by studying this phenomenon.

We approached Seattle in the rain to no one's surprise. The Cessna landed in minor turbulence with a soft bounce and a short slide at the Boeing airfield just south of the city. Other than a few words of comfort from the paramedics, the flight had been made in silence. We were startled when the pilot asked, "Anyone see the ambulance?" Apparently we had taxied down the runway in the wrong direction and our ride was waiting at the opposite terminal. After twelve hours, two flights, and three ambulance rides, it seemed fitting that I should have to wait a few more minutes for the final leg of my journey. I actually smiled at the irony as we slowly turned and taxied through the downpour to the other end of the airport.

Harborview Medical Center (HMC) sprawls just off the James Street exit of Interstate 5 northbound. It is a rambling beige behemoth monopolizing the hillside east of downtown Seattle. It commands a stunning view of south Puget Sound, Vashon Island and the city center. Harborview began in 1877 as a welfare hospital for King County. It was moved to the present location in 1931 and established connections with the University of Washington School of Medicine in 1945. The hospital remains a major teaching site for all health sciences and is a Level I trauma center for the region. It is owned by the residents of King County and managed by the University.

Like most hospitals built in its time, Harborview's central tower once contained all the essentials required for good medical care. Technology exploded into medicine and along with it the size, sophistication, and cost of equipment skyrocketed. Entire floors, nay wings, of buildings were devoted to specialized laboratories, diagnostic suites, and the patients they were designed to serve.

As hospitals became increasingly more compartmentalized, patients became more segregated. Architecturally this change was manifested by the haphazard addition of towers and ells connected to the original structure by an exasperating maze of walkways and tunnels. HMC was no exception as it spread in three dimensions to fill all available topographic space. Its progeny even crossed Ninth Avenue to occupy several additional buildings.

It was the ground-floor emergency room of this imposing structure at which I arrived just after midnight on April 21. The first face I saw through a drugged fog was the haggard visage of my husband. He gave me an awkward hug as the gurney was rolled down the hallway and into a minuscule curtained-off cubicle. We had little privacy for our emotional reunion as institutional personnel scurried around processing admission information.

Robert had arrived at HMC only ten minutes before I did. He had made the return trip from Oregon in record time, stopping only to make arrangements for his son, Brian, to stay with friends overnight.

Robert and I knew the technical fine points of my malfunction and most of the scenarios for possible outcomes. I don't know if that information made it easier or harder for us to deal with the gravity of the situation. Our being physicians gave us profound insight into what was to come but put us at some disadvantage as well. The neurosurgeons often treated us as equals rather than patient and spouse, thus depriving us of some explanations which they took for granted we would understand. Having endured almost three days of this nightmare in solitude, I longed for compassion and physical contact rather than didacticism.

No matter; it was Robert's dear face and eyes clouded with concern that I most wanted to see. I felt an immense load lifted from my shoulders now that I no longer had to carry the responsibility of my outcome alone. It was comforting to be enfolded in his protective arms and give up trying to control my fate. A chain of disease unfolding had been set in motion and the aneurysm affair would march on to its inevitable conclusion. In the days to come all my energies would be applied to the process of survival.

An answer to prayer is what a miracle is.

I languished in the emergency room while Robert filled out forms. A brusque junior medical student showed up to obtain my history. He seemed to find a significantly shortened rendition to his liking. The young extern proceeded with a physical evaluation that was also abbreviated by the fact that everyone already knew what was wrong with me.

My admission chart would read: THE PATIENT IS A 51-YEAR OLD WOMAN PHYSICIAN, FOUR DAYS STATUS POST GRADE II SUBARACHNOID HEMORRHAGE SECONDARY TO A RUPTURED LEFT PICA ANEURYSM. CURRENTLY THE PATIENT IS GLASGOW COMA SCALE 15, ALERT AND ORIENTED X 4, NONFOCAL WITH COMPLAINT ONLY OF MODERATE HEADACHE. Moderate, my ass!

After 400 milligrams of morphine I could only wish!

The emergency department of HMC was very busy even at midnight. I was only one of many disasters needing attention. After almost two hours of anxious waiting an orderly arrived to roll me down to Radiology for my third CAT scan. He was dressed in a wrinkled white uniform. I noticed that there was blood splattered on his shoes. He looked tired. I *was* tired. We did not speak.

The receiving area of Radiology was overflowing. Patients were parked in the hallways, covered with blankets, with their IV poles leaning precariously from the rails of their mobile beds. Here and there an arm or a foot stuck out from beneath its cover. Scattered soft moans could be heard. Other patients sat slumped over in wheelchairs, looking like stumps; forlorn and abandoned. They were wearing an assortment of bandages, casts, and monitoring cables. I joined their ranks with my gurney stationed anonymously against a wall. Some of the more alert patients probably wondered what I was doing there—I looked so normal on the outside.

After the CAT scan the same disheveled aide returned me to the emergency ward without comment. I was exhausted. After a short resettlement in the ER I returned to Radiology for my second arteriogram. Despite all the records my Idaho physicians had sent with me, the staff of HMC wanted their own for verification. Harborview's angiography room was just as cold as the one in Boise; the sensations of heat and flashing lights just as intense. This time, thanks to morphine, I slept through much of the procedure and awoke being transferred into a bed in the Neurosurgery

Intensive Care Unit (Neuro ICU). My doctors assured me that the room had a great view of the harbor. It was now the small hours of Monday morning.

My family arrived in Seattle from Boise at noontime. Hiliary and Jessica had been briefed on my illness by their father who then shepherded them and himself and his wife, Susie, into a downtown hotel for the duration of the immediate crisis. Troy and I had become friends in the years following our breakup and his support of the children was invaluable.

I woke up in the evening to find my two best friends standing at the bedside. Dr. Joan Hulme, fellow neonatologist, had been a senior medical student, then Pediatric intern and resident and post-doctoral fellow at the University of Utah during my tenure 1976-1980. In some ways I considered her my protégée while she thought of me more as an older sister. Joanie had an arm around Kay Hendrix, an NICU respiratory therapist whose friendship extended back to my year at Brookwood Hospital in Birmingham in 1981. Kay had taken the first available flight out of Alabama as soon as Jessica called her on Monday morning.

These seven people dearest to me roamed the halls of Harborview. They lounged all over the waiting room and went out to lunch and waited. And waited. In a distressed cluster the Margaret Watkins' support group attended family information sessions and discussed the medical aspects of my case. The two men and five women snacked from vending machines and tried to rest on the well worn furniture outside the Neuro ICU. When they came to my bedside in pairs I tried to listen to their words of encouragement although I often abruptly fell asleep in mid conversation.

My primary care nurse worked a twelve-hour day shift, so she organized the myriad details of my technology governed existence. Colleen was exuberant and indefatigable and had wild red hair to match her personality. She was firm but compassionate with me and my visitors. I knew I would be in good hands after my operation.

The neurosurgery residents dropped in sporadically for their version of a social visit which usually lasted for three minutes or less. They brought more forms and papers for me to read and sign. I was drugged and in pain and did not care much about the fine print. Robert read everything carefully and gave me a summary of the main points.

"Just give me the bottom line, Dear," I said with weary resignation.

The consent form for surgery was broad in scope and vague in detail. It mentioned almost in passing the possibility that I might die during the operation or as a complication of it. But heck, I knew that already!

Doctor Tandin was one of the senior residents assigned to my case. For a head cracker he had a surprisingly upbeat attitude. He was really cute, in an exotic Far East sort of way. I immediately decided to cooperate with him and win an ally. He seemed particularly concerned about my hair. Several times in our brief discussions Dr. Tandin returned to the issue of shaving my head. He suggested that I go for a Mohawk hairstyle or a front flap as only the left lower quadrant of my scalp had to be impeccably bald.

"Shave it all, and let's get on with it!" I snapped, forgetting my resolution to be charming.

My primary surgeon, Dr. H. Richard Winn, appeared on the scene only rarely. Even though he was the force behind the proceedings, he left all of the mundane decisions to the housestaff (physicians in training). When we first met in the emergency room I was unimpressed with Dick Winn. I expected Goliath. I got David instead. This slender balding man was to be my savior; he of the calm demeanor and steady hands. Right away I noticed his short well-groomed fingernails. I liked that. Those hands would soon be in my brain.

I slid in and out of narcotic nirvana as the night passed and the light of Tuesday morning, April 22, crept into the room with a view. Robert and I tried to talk about matters of the heart. He sat near my bed and we held hands tightly amid the trappings of technology. Our mournful gazing at each other said all the things we could not verbally express.

As the noon hour approached there was a great purposeful bustle in the Neuro ICU in preparation for my departure to the operating room. Colleen directed the siege while my loved ones sneaked in for a final hug and prayer. I felt as if they had come to say goodbye. Perhaps they had. As my familiar gurney and I rolled into the elevator Robert started crying.

CHAPTER 12

UP TO THE LINE

The adult human brain weighs roughly three pounds. It looks a bit like an oyster-colored head of cauliflower and has the texture of a fresh mushroom. The three membranes (meninges) covering it are transparent and glistening, making the small veins that fan out over the surface readily visible. The brain is both more and less fragile than you might imagine and infinitely more complicated.

PATIENT #2-07-94-82 WAS BROUGHT TO THE OPERATING ROOM WHERE SHE WAS IDENTIFIED BY WRIST BRACELET. PATIENT SUCCESSFULLY UNDERWENT LEFT LATERAL SUBOCCIPITAL CRANIECTOMY FOR CLIPPING OF PICA ANEURYSM. ALSO INSTALLATION OF LEFT FRONTAL CAMINO INTRACRANIAL PRESSURE MONITOR. THE ENTIRE HEAD WAS CLEANED IN

THE USUAL MANNER AND WRAPPED IN KERLIX.
Surgeons: Winn, Skirboll, Santiago.

As dictated into the medical record, this was a summary of the summary of the operation. It was a forty-nine-word condensation of thirteen hours of general anesthesia and surgery. During this time I had my head shaved; a catheter inserted into my spinal canal; a catheter placed in my bladder; a rubber hose through my nose into my stomach; a large plastic tube slipped through my vocal cords for breathing; and my head skewered into fixation with a tripod Mayfield holder. And this was all before surgery even got underway.

Dr. Skirboll made an incision along my spine from the top of my shoulders to the base of my skull and then arched it over to my left ear. Using a Bovie electrocautery unit he burned his way through layers of muscles and their connective tissues. A COUPLE OF MUSCLES WERE LEFT ON THE OCCIPUT FOR ATTACHMENT LATER. He ronguered a two-inch hole in my skull down to the brain. Further burrowing and bone removal at last revealed the aneurysm bulging from the medial surface of an artery leading into the left side of my cerebellum. THE CRANIAL NERVES COULD BE SEEN IN THE SUPERIOR AND LATERAL PORTIONS OF THE OPERATING FIELD.

At this stage of the surgical agenda Dr. Winn arrived on the scene to use the operating microscope. The tension in the room became palpable as the defect bulged into Dr. Winn's field of view. There was a BIT OF BLEEDING requiring some quick action by the surgical team to regain hemodynamic control as another unit of blood began infusing into my veins. After some delicate dissecting Dr. Winn placed a

Sugita clip around the neck of the aneurysm and clamped it tight. A second clip was placed in parallel to the first to insure against further hemorrhaging.

After generous washing and packing of the surgical field, Dr. Skirboll retraced his steps, putting the pieces of the back of my head back together as best he could. For the rip in the outer meninges, the dura, he used a patch made from the heart sac of a cow.

During these twelve operative hours I had been positioned on my right side. Not quite finished yet, Dr. Santiago rolled me over onto my back and drilled a hole in my skull about three inches above my forehead. Through this hole he placed a titanium bolt that housed a pressure transducer. This system would keep track of the pressure inside my skull in case there was swelling or further bleeding that might impinge on my brain.

THE PATIENT TOLERATED THE PROCEDURE WELL AND THERE WERE NO COMPLICATIONS. During the operation I lost four pints of blood and received two in return plus nineteen pints of various other fluids.

I arrived back in Colleen's domain looking like the Pillsbury Doughboy who had been attacked with crochet hooks.

How much do I remember about my stay in the neurosurgery intensive care unit? Too much!

The first clear sensation I had following the operation was a feeling of swimming upward through some heavy and murky liquid much like mercury. Then I burst into consciousness with a horrible realization of what had happened to me. I felt like an ax had been wedged in the middle of my skull. I was absolutely panicked by feelings of helplessness and a misplaced sense of betrayal. I wanted my mother!

My terror and agony must have been apparent in my groaning and thrashing about. The nurses asked me if I was in pain. I responded with as vigorous an affirmative nod as I could muster. A bolus of morphine sent me into a blessed period of unconsciousness.

I awoke for brief moments of lucidity that allowed me to acknowledge the hospital staff and visitors. My family was ecstatic.

An answer to prayer is what a miracle is.

My voice was hoarse from having had a breathing tube through my vocal cords. The skin was so stretched over my swollen body that it was shiny. My eyelids would scarcely separate.

Late in the first postoperative day the surgeons made their rounds, checking on the condition of their ICU patients.

Dr. Tandin was disgustingly cheerful when he asked, "Dr. Watkins! How are you feeling?"

I considered saying truthfully that I felt like road kill but settled instead for a sarcastic reply, "Just peachy keen!"

My response got a chuckle from the neurosurgery entourage and was the first sign of humor I had seen any of them display.

Protocols existed for following neurologically insulted patients to ascertain the status of their nervous system. Every two hours the Neuro ICU nurses flashed a light in my eyes and pounded on my kneecaps with a rubber hammer to check my reflexes. Twice daily my physicians would ask me the date and day of the week, my name and location, and other inane questions to determine if I indeed knew who and where I was. It was difficult for me to keep track of the days and I had not a clue to the time since I was unable to read the clock. I must have answered questions reasonably well for the neurosurgery residents would all smile and depart in a flock.

Thinking that the worst of the ordeal was over, my family had a celebration of sorts. They went to an expensive restaurant for dinner. The women treated themselves to a shopping trip to the Pike Street Marketplace, a Seattle landmark. Their jubilation was short lived.

All lightheartedness evaporated a day later. Every four hours an ultrasound technician would rub lubricating gel over my smooth scalp and run a Doppler probe around my skull. The sonar-like waves reflected patterns onto the screen that showed my doctors how well blood was flowing in the arteries in my brain, including the one with the clipped aneurysm protruding from its bifurcation. This day things were not going well.

The small blood vessels were reacting to the irritation of bleeding and the manipulation of surgery by constricting, thereby drastically reducing blood flow to the left side of my brain. A second wave of intense concern washed over my family as Dr. Winn explained to them the potentially deadly complication of vasospasm. Unless this process could be reversed I would likely die from an ischemic infarct. Most medical options had already been utilized to their utmost benefit. It was Dr. Winn's recommendation that cerebral angioplasty be undertaken as a last resort.

Angioplasty is an attempt to open a normal but spasmed artery (or a structurally narrowed one) by stretching the constricted portion in minuscule increments using an intravascular balloon. For the cerebral circulation these balloons are incredibly small. They are positioned in the brain via techniques similar to those used for arteriograms. This would be the third time that flexible silicon tubes had found their way from the top of my leg to the top of my head.

One of the nation's best invasive neuroradiologists worked at the University of Washington School of Medicine. With incredibly delicate skill he had rescued patients in my predicament. Cerebral angioplasty was a risky undertaking with no guarantees, but Dr. Joe Eskridge was the one to call upon in such desperate circumstances.

Robert had to grapple with medical decisions as I could no longer voice my opinion. We had discussed resuscitation and life-support issues at length so he understood how I felt about existing in a nonfunctional state. My family knew that I had documents signed for living will/durable power of attorney and that I wished to be an organ donor. So I believe it was with minimal hesitation that they unanimously agreed to proceed with angioplasty with utmost haste.

I knew very little of what was happening at this point. Colleen informed me that I was going down to the Radiology suite once again for angioplasty. I was already developing a paranoid complex. I was terrified of what my caretakers were planning to do to me next. I begged Colleen not to send me downstairs. I just wanted to be left in relative peace to die if I must.

My previous procedure would pale in comparison to what was in store for me this time. Conversations with my family at this juncture were brief and awful. I know my family said their individual prayers, and

Heaven knows I prayed fervently for myself!

When prayers are answered, a miracle happens.

Once again my family was bivouaced in the waiting room. They had been emotionally ambushed. They wandered the halls aimlessly, polishing their praying skills. My loved ones stood in clusters on the outside patio in the spring air and suffered. Despite the ninety-one years of their combined medical training they could not help me. It was a terrible time for us all.

Wounded animals often crawl off from their herd or pack to heal alone or die alone. At last I understood why this was so. It is instinctual to turn inward all faculties; to concentrate all energy on the healing process. I spent many hours in this state, aware on some primeval level only of my existence. It was like being wrapped in a warm cocoon; being returned to the womb. Cognition brought with it overwhelming pain and the frightening admission of helplessness. I welcomed the peace of oblivion that came with unconsciousness. I simply went away somewhere.

It was in this state of withdrawal that I had a near-death experience. It occurred during the angioplasties when vasospasm threatened my cognitive person and the risk of an arterial rupture in my head put my life at stake. I did not see bright lights nor behold celestial beings. What I did see again with exquisite clarity was the fine line between life and death. It was as graphic to me as an actual line drawn in the dirt. I believe that line represented my river Jordan.

There was a tremendous force drawing me to the other side of this line. I saw, not a darkness, but a soft grayness that was indescribably peaceful. I sensed a power in that grayness that beckoned me but I knew that I must cross the line to find this refuge. I really wanted to go!

There were also forces restraining me in the land of mortals. My guardian angel waited at a distance, giving me the freedom to make a choice between living and dying. It seemed as if I hovered there on the brink of eternity weighing all things in the balance. Robert's incredible love had a major hold on me. I knew that he would let go of me if I chose to cross over that line. The thought of leaving him and my children made me infinitely sad as I stood there longing for a haven that I did not fully comprehend.

A selfish component to my internal deliberations also motivated my return to the virtual world. At age fifty-one I simply was not ready to die. There were many marvelous adventures on this earth just waiting for my participation. I pondered over all these conflicting emotions and then made a deliberate choice. It was with great reluctance that I slowly backed away from the line. I have the reassurance, however, that when I again approach that fine line I will step over it into a glorious peace.

And so it came to pass---my survival. Withdrawn and unresponsive, I hunkered down and waited for healing. Oblivious to the real world, I was not aware that within twelve hours of the angioplasty I lost the ability to move my left arm and leg and constrict my right pupil. My family and friends sank into even deeper despair at the dismal news of more vasospasm. Their prayers increased in fervor and frequency as the neurosurgeons started an intravenous drip of Neosynephrine that rocketed my blood pressure near to 300 mmHg. My doctors were hoping to force open the arteries in my brain before my entire vascular system had a terminal blowout.

Once again a miracle happened.

Awakening from the second procedure was like a return trip to Hell. Knowing that my body had been sorely insulted by another twelve hours of anesthesia and manipulation, the doctors chose to keep me heavily sedated and on a respirator. Regaining consciousness with a large plastic tube down my trachea was my worst nightmare coming true. I did not conduct myself well. I wiggled and squirmed. I chewed on the tube. I pulled at adhesive tape and wires until the staff had no choice but to tie my hands and feet to the bed rails.

The combination of stress and drugs produced the first of many vivid hallucinations. I became a large green rat from the planet Saturn. With my three little red eyes I glared balefully at anyone approaching me. I would gladly have ripped to shreds anything I could have gotten my paws on. This was my first experience with narcotic induced psychosis but it would not be my last.

There were two things about this stage of post-operative care that I really, really hated. The respirator used was state-of-the-art and responded within milliseconds to my demand for air. From my battered point of view even this minuscule delay filled me with panic. I felt like I was suffocating. I found myself anticipating the machine's cycle even though I knew it was waiting for a signal from me before it would inflate my lungs with oxygen. "Fighting the ventilator" is the medical phrase used to describe my agitation and lack of synchronization. I am sure the nurses were grateful when their unruly patient no longer required a respirator.

The second thing I detested was the breathing tube

anchored to the side of my face by layers of adhesive tape. It passed through my vocal cords into the upper part of my trachea. It produced a sensation of intense pressure in the back of my throat and triggered my gag and cough reflexes. The nurses used a long pliable catheter about the size of a straw to suction my tube. They first injected a small amount of sterile saline to loosen mucus. I felt as if I were drowning even though the volume was insignificant. As the suction catheter passed beyond the tip of the tube and touched my airway, I felt as if a bolt of lightning had struck the center of my chest and exited through the top of my head. I coughed, all right! You bet I did!

I was still in the mood to rip something apart. It slowly dawned on me that dying wasn't all that hard. It was the struggle to come back to life that hurt.

After the hateful tube was removed my throat felt like it had been sandblasted. My voice was barely audible and would remain soft and raspy for weeks to come. I became increasingly irritable and defensive and paranoid. Whenever anyone entered the room I flinched, wondering what new tortures awaited me. The patient in the room with a view was becoming her own monster.

The nurses turned me in bed every four hours. They propped up various parts of me with pillows and offered what comfort they could. I ached in muscles I had not thought about since anatomy classes in medical school.

I developed a peculiar little ritual that I performed each time I awoke. I made an inventory of all my tubes, monitors and catheters. Perhaps I needed confirmation that they were still in the right places. At this time my accoutrements included a bladder catheter, two intravenous lines attached to arm veins, a large rubber tube down one nostril into my stomach, a large catheter going into the subclavian vein beneath my right collarbone, and a small catheter in the artery in my right wrist. How could I overlook my least favorite---the pressure bolt sticking straight up out of my skull above my left eye!

It had now been ten days since I had received any nutrition other than intravenously. My stomach rebelled when tube feedings were started and I added nausea to my list of complaints. The Ensure, a high calorie liquid, was cold when it hit my stomach, having bypassed the usual warming-up stages of mouth and esophagus. I soon came to dislike feeding time. I had no appetite and was unaware of how thin I had become. The time arrived when I felt particularly defensive and pulled out the annoying feeding tube, tape and all. The nurses were not pleased.

Food intake would prove to be a major struggle for weeks to come. The first meal tray arrived from the cafeteria. I had never seen anything look as appealing as the green salad piled high with croutons and dressing. I attacked it with zeal but soon found that my jaws and tongue seemed to have minds of their own. Nothing worked according to the signals I was sending. The muscles on the left side of my tongue were very weak so I kept biting the tip of it. Soon the insides of my cheeks were also gnawed to pulp. After a few bites I gave up in despair.

What little rest I got was constantly being interrupted. I began to have paranoid ideas secondary to sleep deprivation and these added to my narcotic neuroses. The patience of my caretakers was seriously challenged. It was to their credit that an air of professional tolerance was maintained. Colleen's occasional scolding kept me from getting totally out of line.

At some point Dr. Santiago removed the bolt from my skull. I simply found it missing from my inventory one day. The subclavian catheter and arterial line were the next tethers to go. I had more freedom to move around but still found it impossible to get comfortable. The large hospital pillows continued to be useless except to prop up body parts since my neck and the back of my head were intolerant to touch.

I swore off narcotics. Two weeks on high dose morphine was virtually making me crazy. I awoke from naps with that horrifying feeling of swimming through thick fluid. My movements were in slow motion as if the mercury had somehow seeped into all my joints. I hated that sensation. The staff offered codeine-based analgesics but I elected to go with Tylenol and sweat it out. Living with pain was preferable to becoming a neurotic nut.

I gradually became more aware of my surroundings: the unused television; the color of the walls; the boom box and tapes I never heard; the window with the great view that I would never look through. By sliding into an S-shape, I could see the clock to my immediate left. It did not appear to be a rational clock. There were too many numbers and too many hands. Sometimes the hands were moving backward. Drugs will do that to you.

My diet was altered to liquids and soft foods. Eating became less of a struggle but still exhausted me. Ensure became my mainstay. I longed for a cup of coffee, hot enough to melt metal.

I was always cold. Neuro ICU staff and visitors seemed comfortable enough. Of course they were scurrying around fully clothed. In contrast I was wearing a flimsy gown that covered only my front on the best of days. My blankets were neatly folded at the foot of the bed where I could not possibly reach them. I attempted and failed to draw up the blankets with my feet. They certainly weren't going to rise up and cover me by their own free will.

Sleep was an elusive escape in the Neuro ICU. I resented anyone who interrupted what little respite I found. Nursing procedures and doctors' rounds seemed to constantly interfere with my body's urgent request for rest. If more than one activity was taking place in my room I became agitated and grumpy. No television or radio for me. Minor discomforts were disproportionately annoying. My skin was as dry as parchment---I looked like I was molting. My breath smelled terrible and I felt like my teeth were wearing little sweaters. Lemon-flavored glycerin swabs left my mouth feeling less like the bottom of a bird cage.

A gentle sponge bath by the nurses was a major treat even over the painful sites of previous venipunctures. With a hose hanging out of my nose and fluid lines running into both arms, I still appreciated a little cosmetic enhancement. Bad hair days were certainly not a problem since I was as bald as an egg.

The entire left side of my scalp was numb. It was weird to rub my hand over my slick pate and feel as if my head ended at midline. My hearing was also affected. Sounds were resonant and seemed amplified.

My underlying mild tinnitus had been greatly exaggerated by the surgery and a loud humming now rendered my left ear useless.

After thirteen days I was stable enough to be transferred from the intensive care unit. Dr. Skirboll removed stitches from the surgical incision and I spent some time getting reacquainted with my bald and now unencumbered head. I tried to express my appreciation to the nursing staff for participating in my preservation. Apologies for the times when I had been insufferable seemed insufficient compensation for their tireless dedication.

I realized with a jolt that I was actually afraid to leave the ICU. What if the staff on the ward did not realize that I could not eat well? What if they expected me to get out of bed when I could hardly roll over in it? What if I needed to use a bed pan and no one was available to help me? I still had a bladder catheter and what if it got kinked or fell out? The constant observation in the Neuro ICU had become a security blanket even as I chaffed at the lack of privacy. I would have to learn how to take care of myself.

I was in the midst of an anxiety attack as a gurney and I were wheeled down a maze of corridors to my new residence. Unknown to me then, Colonel Robbins was arriving at Harborview to begin his own descent into a medical maelstrom.

CHAPTER 13
A MEDICAL FURBALL

When the helicopter deposited him on the painted white cross of Harborview Medical Center's helipad, the jet jockey was once again hustled into the emergency ward and subjected to another battery of exhausting tests, including repeat CAT scan and arteriogram. Apparently the medical team at HMC wanted their own specialized examinations despite the excellent records transferred from MAMC with their patient.

The colonel was not in pain but he still had no vision. The usual bevy of students and neurosurgical residents filed through his cubicle with their questions and papers and pinpricks. Finally Dr. David Newell, the attending staff neurosurgeon and Dr. Winn's associate, sat down beside Mike and laid out the complexities of his condition.

As the late hours of Friday night passed in a blur of

tests and a barrage of information, the pilot dealt with the news of his malady in his usual objective, methodical, check-list fashion. The first steps in defeating an enemy were to identify it and assess its weaknesses. As far as he could tell, albeit with limited knowledge, aneurysms had no weaknesses.

"Well. Then fix the damn thing and be on with it!" Mike told Dr. Newell. He was worried more about his continuing inability to see than about the intricate and potentially deadly operation itself.

Chris Robbins and his sister Mandy arrived at Harborview filled with anxiety. They found Mike subdued but optimistic. Tears of relief soon mixed with those of uncertainty as the children watched their father being wheeled from the Neurosurgical Intensive Care Unit to the elevator to begin his descent into the nightmare of brain surgery.

Two floors above the operating suite, the recently vacated room with a view in the Neuro ICU was cleaned and restocked and ready for its new occupant's hoped-for return. As I struggled to eat dinner on Three West, Colonel Robbins' body temperature hit 90 degrees Fahrenheit. The carefully controlled hypothermia would lower his metabolic rate and decrease the oxygen requirements of his brain tissue. This reduction would allow his body to better withstand the fourteen hours of general anesthesia and extensive vascular manipulations that were to follow.

After the usual preparations of ventricular pressure monitors and drains and spinal canal catheters, Mike's frame was rolled into prone position and his head was skewered in three-point fixation in a Mayfield holder. Then Drs. Skirboll and Newell began their dissection at the base of his skull. A twelve-inch T-shaped incision was made through skin and muscle using scapel, cautery, and blunted scrapers. The wound extended from ear to ear and down Mike's neck to his shoulders. Bone crushers and ronguers soon made short work of the arch of his first cervical vertebra.

The large dissecting aneurysm on the colonel's right vertebral artery had not yet ruptured. Its over-distended wall was pulsating with malignant hemorrhagic potential with every beat of Mike's cooled-down heart. A thin muslin sling was wrapped around the artery for several centimeters, enclosing the proximal and distal portions of the defect in a snug cocoon of safety. The location of the aneurysm precluded any attempt to place a clip on it.

On the officer's left vertebral artery the aneurysm was tattered around the rupture site. A mass of clotted blood served notice of its recent explosion. Mike's journey toward that final fine line had been much closer to reality than he could have imagined. The now-deflated neck of the aneurysm was trapped between two straight Sugita clips, thus neutralizing its deadly threat of re-bleeding.

On their way out of his skull, the neurosurgeons closed Mike's brain covering with a dural bovine pericardial patch. The ANG officer and I now shared a similar history and a piece of cow heart in our heads. The stricken pilot received twelve quarts of intravenous fluids and two units of blood during surgery. Before Mike even left the operating room his body had begun to swell.

In her occupation as a speech therapist, Maria Subra had worked extensively with stroke patients as they struggled with rehabilitation issues such as loss of speech, amnesia, and paralysis of any number of muscle groups. She had patients who had survived ruptured aneurysms in various portions of their neuroanatomy, and she knew well what handicaps they had to overcome. It was with complete surprise and utter dismay, however, that she learned on May 5 that just such a calamity had befallen her dear friend in Tacoma.

Maria arrived at Harborview in the late evening. She was greeted by Chris and Mandy in the same waiting room that my family had so recently invaded. The Robbins' support group would go through their own anguish and uncertainty as the colonel's strong constitution buckled down to the job of survival.

Maria thought she was prepared to see her friend under maximum duress but her heart almost stopped at the sight of him. He was bloated beyond recognition and festooned with a jungle of tubes, wires, catheters, IVs, cables; and slender metal poles with curved limbs to hold them all. She cried when she saw him despite her resolve.

The jet pilot was unaware of the effect his appearance had on his children and Maria. He fought his way to consciousness from an anesthetic stupor only to realize that he was still intubated and freezing. He hated being strapped down but was oblivious to the fact that he had put himself in restraints by his combativeness and repeated attempts to remove his breathing tube.

Mike was occasionally cognizant enough to realize that his vision had returned seemingly unimpaired. He gratefully acknowledged the warm blankets the nurses placed over him when they saw him shivering. For days he awoke to periods of abject misery and sank ambivalently into a morass of narcotic nightmares. A mild degree of vasospasm developed on the fourth post-operative day, but it slowly resolved without discernible residual effects. The staff continued to push fluids into his distended veins and Ensure down his feeding tube to make certain that his body stayed over-hydrated and reasonably nourished.

The resiliency of the human body is truly astounding. The ability of the trillions of cells in our physical plant to heal themselves is its own miracle. The complex metabolic mechanisms that repair and sustain our being are interrelated in overlapping protective pathways that bring the human body back to a state of wellness from even the most grievous injuries.

The military man experienced this well orchestrated reconstruction as he lived in a haze of drugs and misery in the Neuro ICU while his battered body slowly mended. The sides of the garish incision at the back of his head slowly knitted together as the surgical wound filled in with granulations that coalesced into scar tissue. Mike's neck would forever remain stiff and uncooperative as a result of this assault.

The first hint that perhaps the pilot had not escaped unscathed from his disaster came on the second day after surgery when his breathing tube was removed. Initially Mike could breathe normally. He sent a heartfelt prayer skyward to St. Michael in thanks for his deliverance from the hated device. His relief was short lived.

The four cranial nerves most caudal on the brainstem control a variety of muscle functions. Among these are muscles that vibrate the vocal cords for the production of sound and ones that raise the cords like drawbridges to allow for breathing. In Mike's case these nerves had sustained some bruising during surgery as they had been pulled to the side of the operating field and anchored out of the way. The pilot's left vocal cord was not receiving proper neural signals so it flapped shut like a trap door.

After an hour of unfettered time the pilot began gasping for air. The endotracheal tube was promptly replaced and his respiratory distress was instantly relieved. Mike's obvious dependency on the tube to keep his airway open depressed him severely.

Since he was unable to speak with the tube in position between his vocal cords, the colonel expressed his needs via a small chalk board. He was to become very proficient in this method of alternative communication. He remained upbeat on the surface but shared some of his angst with Maria. Later she remarked, "Mike never once has felt sorry for himself."

After two more failed attempts at removing the endotracheal tube from their patient, there remained no choice for the neurosurgeons but to place a semi-permanent opening into Mike's airway. This tracheostomy hole was located just below his Adam's apple. Through it he could breathe and cough just fine but there was no air passing through his vocal cords to make sounds. The military man dealt with this complication in his usual implacable manner. The medical profession tuned up their patient a bit more and transferred him to a step-down unit on May 15.

In the transitional unit the fighter jet pilot dealt with the harsh realities of being grounded. He quickly learned how to properly care for the half-inch hole in his neck. In good spirits he coped with swallowing difficulties and worked his way through the usual repertory of pureed foods and liquid supplements. Therapists coached him in exercises designed to strengthen throat and tongue muscles gone slack from enervation.

Mike's family and friends returned to their routines as the colonel tried to remember how to dress himself. Tying his shoelaces remained a task beyond his capabilities. It seemed hopelessly complicated to him although he knew he had laced up and tied his military boots five thousand times before.

Mike forgot the names of his children although he could recognize their faces. The staff of HMC came to the conclusion that their patient would require an extended period of hospitalization and rehabilitation. They tried to prepare him for placement in a nursing home but he balked totally at the idea.

After three weeks under siege at Harborview, the ANG officer was transferred back into the embrace of Madigan Army Medical Center. It was now nearing Memorial Day and his trials were far from over.

CHAPTER 14

TRANSITION

Three West was optimistically known as The Floor. A patient had moved up several notches on the probability-of-survival list in order to be transferred there from the Neurosurgical Intensive Care Unit. As the gurney was being rolled down the corridors the bright fluorescent lights and acoustical tiles passing over me were like scenes from a bad movie.

I was still emotionally agitated about the idea of being alone. From a positive point of view, my family would have more liberal visiting hours and I would certainly have more privacy. The flip side to all these benefits was that I would have to assume more responsibility for my own care. My greatest apprehension was that on this particular Friday the staff on The Floor would decide that I should get up and get moving for the weekend. I wasn't sure that I could even sit up, let alone go for a stroll. I had already formed a bad opinion of Three West before the elevator doors even opened onto The Floor.

I was fortunate to have a small private room after two weeks of having every bodily function on full display in the Neuro ICU. The nursing aide opened the drapes in my new space and proclaimed that I had a great view. Whoopie!

The thing I wanted most was sleep. My room was tucked away at the end of the hall and there was little disturbance. I could hear voices and phones at the central nurses' station. The carpet cushioned foot traffic to the stairwell and the elevator was at the opposite end of the corridor. People could no longer pop into my room unannounced since the door clicked loudly when it was opened. This small victory over invasion of privacy gave me my first taste of independence in thirteen long days.

The nurses bustled around my bed taking my vital signs and measuring intravenous fluid rates and urine output. Perhaps they recorded my appearance-- PALE AND GAUNT--and disposition--PEEVISH. The lunch hour came and went without my participation. Apparently I had left the ICU too early and arrived on The Floor too late for meal delivery. It really did not matter as my eating efforts were still mostly unsuccessful.

There are a series of incredibly important large nerves that extend in twelve split pairs from the underside of the brain. Called the *cranial nerves*, they control neural functions as diverse as the sense of smell and movement of the diaphragm. The hindmost of these nerves exit the brain beneath the cerebellum. In my case numbers eight through twelve on the left side had taken a direct hit from the surgery and the vasospasm. I could not swallow without choking because my throat muscles were weak and my left vocal cord was paralyzed. I still craved lettuce but the rest of my appetite remained indifferent.

When the evening shift started a beam of bright light burst into my room shortly after three p.m. in the form of Johnny. This vigorous and compassionate young man soon had my room and its occupant spiffed up for inspection. He inquired after my needs, brought fresh water with ice, and discreetly replaced soiled linens. Then he left me in peace, promising to return and help me with dinner.

I napped fitfully, dreaming darkly. When meatloaf appeared with all its trimmings and caramel custard, I viewed the tray with mixed emotions.

True to his word, Johnny arrived with a positive outlook and a bib. He coaxed his reluctant patient into swallowing green peas and applesauce by encouraging me with each spoonful as though I were a child. After the meatloaf was minced and mixed into a slurry with gravy and mashed potatoes, a few bites of it glided past my wounded throat.

"Part of your problem," Johnny declared, "is your debilitation. We are going to work on that while you are here in transition." He kindly refrained from mentioning my obdurate attitude. My zealous and handsome young nurse took on as a personal challenge the goal of having me fatter and more upright by the end of the weekend.

I slept very little that first night on The Floor.

There was a large clock on the wall at the foot of my bed. The second hand moved jerkily along its predestined path as the minutes ticked by interminably. I was visited this night by the first of the dark specters; these were paranoid delusions resulting from narcotic withdrawal. I did not yet know that this psychological mayhem would deprive me of sleep far more effectively than my physical ailments would.

Sleep deprivation would prove to add its own dimension of dementia. Personnel entering my room now took on the nature of adversaries sent there to insure my discomfort. It was hard to be civil to the night shift as I misinterpreted their interruptions. The patient in room 314 was becoming her own nightmare.

When at last the sun came up on Saturday I was awake to witness its arrival. I still had a bladder catheter and an intravenous line but those were soon removed by the nurse on day shift. I was at last unencumbered.

The moment finally arrived when I was desperate enough to make the twenty-foot trip to the bathroom. Robert helped me swing my feet over the side of the bed. I had a moment of absolute panic when the bottoms of my feet hit the floor. I felt as if thousands of little pins were pricking my soles. Robert stood in front of me while I maintained a death grip on the front of his shirt. We inched toward the toilet in an awkward shuffle.

"Don't leave me!" I implored, as my husband stepped away to open the door to the bathroom. With a gentle chuckle he submitted to my vise-like reattachment to his garment.

I was embarrassed to urinate and have a bowel movement with Robert hovering nearby to prevent me from falling off the commode, but he seemed totally unfazed.   Resuming our bizarre slow waltz, we maneuvered our way to the sink. After washing my hands I took a deep breath and raised my eyes to the mirror.

I got a good look at myself for the first time in sixteen days. I was not prepared for the thinness and pallor of my face. I hardly recognized the gaunt bald stranger staring at me with sunken tormented eyes. I had never really wondered what I would look like with no hair. I was surprised to see that my skull was strangely shaped and that my ears were different sizes and stuck out from my head at odd angles.

There was a ten-inch angry red scar running up the center of my neck and curving behind my left ear. I could see it clearly reflected in the hand mirror Joan had left for me. I stared at my wound with morbid appraisal and ran my fingers gently along its sore ruffled edges. I could see and feel an egg-size soft swelling behind my ear just below the puckered zipper of the scar. When I pressed on this mass it was filled with fluid and tender. I would learn later that this liquid was leaking through a hole in the outer covering of my brain and causing much of the pain in my neck that continued to plague me.

A few minutes in front of the mirror satisfied my curiosity and my husband shuffled me back into bed. Afterwards I never gave much thought to my appearance and none of my visitors commented upon the lopsided construction of my cranium.

Johnny continued as my evening angel. I adored him and meekly followed his instructions. Shortly after his weekend shift began, Johnny arrived in my room with an armload of towels and announced blithely that I would be taking a shower.

"You've got to be kidding!" I said, with no small degree of alarm. He wasn't.

I soon found myself creeping to the bathroom once more, firmly attached to Johnny's uniform. He gently helped me out of the hospital gown and onto a plastic stool in the midst of heavenly clouds of steam in the shower. It was the most memorable bath of my life.

Johnny wrapped me in several large towels and practically carried me to the bed. Temperature control was just one of many homeostatic mechanisms yet to be reestablished in my body. I found myself shivering uncontrollably. Still in the nude I rattled my way between the sheets. Johnny added a heap of blankets fresh from the warmer.

A great weariness overtook me. I had a short dreamless nap followed by another installment of the war against malnutrition. I endeavored to increase my caloric intake by ordering every dessert on the hospital menu.

A dietician came to review my meal plans. She added high protein milkshakes and pureed fruits to the daily selections. I still wanted a tossed salad but settled for ranch dressing on mashed potatoes. I squirreled away nonperishable goodies under my pillow and munched constantly. Cartons of milk and Ensure and fruit juice were assembled on the bedside table like ranks of toy soldiers. Grapes required very little chewing and they fast became my favorite snack.

A speech therapist worked with me daily to improve the quality of my voice. She gave me exercises to strengthen my throat and tongue muscles. I slowly stopped drooling and biting myself. When I stuck my tongue out, it deviated sharply to the left because of muscle and nerve damage. My children apparently found this trait quite amusing and requested frequent demonstrations.

One of the few joys of my days on The Floor was a return visit from my daughters. Jessica had just finished her freshman year at BSU and was considering moving to her first apartment. Hiliary brought marvelous pictures from her senior prom the week before. Her high school graduation was three weeks away. I promised to be at the ceremony if possible, but at the moment I doubted my ability to even traverse the outside corridor.

The girls read to me from books and newspapers. Hiliary helped me with dinner and was appalled when I stuffed green peas up my nose to amuse her. The laughter did us good. After that visit, I think my children realized that their mom was truly back in the game. They stopped worrying so much about me and let me resume my maternal prerogative of worrying about them.

I had another angel of mercy named Beverly who worked the night shift. Late one evening I could not rest because of my neck pain. She understood that I wanted no part of the narcotics scene. After several lengthy calls to the neurosurgery resident she obtained an order for an anti-inflammatory drug that did the trick. Beverly was a transplanted southerner like me and her graciousness lingered along with her soft accent. While she was checking me over and filling out my chart one midnight, I asked her how she seemed to know just what I needed without my asking for it.

Beverly related her own time of tribulation. Two

years previously she had been in my same predicament after brain surgery for what proved to be a benign tumor. She understood from experience what patients wanted in terms of comfort measures and moral support. She agreed that the night hours could be a black hole that sucked up the resolve of even the toughest individual. Her commitment to patient care was obvious in her every action. She was a true beacon in the darkness of my worst problem on The Floor.

By this time in my transitional care, narcotic withdrawal and sleep deprivation had let my disturbing delusions run amok. These were most severe at night when I had no distractions. In the midnight hours I searched my room frantically for a bomb that I was convinced would detonate at 3:30 a.m. Finding nothing, I crouched beside the bed as the clock moved slowly toward my fantasized doomsday. I was drenched with sweat when the zero hour finally passed without Armageddon. I collapsed in bed unbelievably relieved and drained. No amount of mental massaging could convince me that I had only imagined the entire debacle.

The room was in shambles. I had dumped out the trash cans and the linen cart in my desperate search for a bomb. All the lights were on and bed covers were strewn everywhere. I was afraid to leave the bed again, sure that terrorists were planning some new infraction. At last I faded out of consciousness as dawn approached. When Beverly awakened me at the end of her shift, the room was all tidied up. She merely squeezed my shoulder and commented that it had been a rough night.

Other than physical and psychic maladjustments, I seemed to be intact. The first hint of possible mental or intellectual impairment was the realization that I could not use the telephone. After picking up the receiver I drew a total blank on how to operate the keypad. The discovery of this mental glitch frightened me and I began to take stock of my other faculties.

My memory seemed to be intact but numbers were a different story. I, who had once recalled dozens of laboratory values on my patients, could now scarcely recall my age; forget about addresses and phone numbers. Since mathematics was never my stellar subject, I concluded that I could function adequately with even more limited abilities in this area. The occupational therapist gave me sequences of numbers to memorize and list on paper. I wrestled with this task halfheartedly.

It continued to be difficult for me to keep time in perspective. I kept referencing everything back to the day of my hemorrhage, April 18th. The cycles of day and night seemed distorted; elongated somehow. My ability to read the clock improved slowly but the absolute value of the hours meant little to me. My world had shrunken to individual units of time: meal time, bath time, therapy time. The world outside the hospital had only vague connections to the reality of my daily struggle with mundane tasks as I gave myself over completely to the role of recovering patient.

When I was a patient did I expect my doctors to be at their best at my bedside? You bet! Dr. Steve Skirboll was the chief resident in neurosurgery when I passed through the intensive care unit. He was two months away from graduation into the world of "real" medicine and showed the weary signs of seven years of training.

Dr. Paul Santiago was large enough to be a

linebacker for the Seattle Seahawks. Occasionally his massive bulk overwhelmed me as he leaned over the bed to change a dressing or tap on my knees with his plexor. It was hard for me to imagine him performing complex neurosurgery with his gigantic hands, but his touch was surprisingly delicate. Dr. Santiago seemed the person most responsible for managing my daily care so I turned on my best cowgirl charm for him.

Many of the residents were young enough to be my children. Even though they were engaged in serious brain business, they were not above practical jokes and friendly scuffling. The physicians made their patient rounds at odd hours, often finding me in various stages of disrepair. The lower ranking trainees followed Dr. Skirboll into the room and clustered at the end of my bed in a housestaff huddle---a medical scrum. The line of students and nurses dribbled out through the door.

I held the housestaff responsible for my day-to-day misery as well as for my recovery. I expected some words of comfort and encouragement as they made their daily assessment. Usually the group had little to say and departed en mass, confirming my impression of the herd effect. I referred to the loosely organized wad as "Alvin and the Chipmunks," but my humor was lost in the flood of their fatigue.

Johnny cajoled and prodded me into getting out of bed. He and the physical therapist took turns helping me walk the hallways. Initially they had to drag me along, supporting most of my weight on their arms and shoulders. I felt like a mop.

With persistence on Johnny's part and perseverance on mine, the day came when I could make the full circle around the nursing station. Wearing Robert's old bath robe I shuffled around the floor proudly, my scalp glowing softly in the harsh light. On my strolls I passed other patients; the walking wounded. They wove their way along the walls, holding on for balance, doing the neurosurgery stagger. In a dazed and befuddled state the post-calamity patients slowly pushed walkers and IV poles up and down the narrow hallways covered in taupe carpet.

The physical therapist rolled a portable staircase up to my door to present me with a new challenge lest I become complacent in my accomplishments. The five steps were insurmountable on my first attempts to climb them. My cheerleader coaxed me into trying one step at a time; up, down, up, down. It seemed as though my knees had forgotten how to bend into right angles. My calf muscles were made of dough. I dutifully struggled to climb the steps three times a day, groaning and muttering all the way to the top.

My temperature instability improved but I continued to have sudden hot flashes and night sweats that led me to shuck clothing and scatter linens helter skelter. In the mornings my room was a wreck despite Beverly's best efforts. Troubling hallucinations continued to bedevil me nightly and added to the mayhem of my transition. The staff on The Floor began to look forward to the day that room 314 was no longer occupied.

Two days after my move onto The Floor, the neurosurgery entourage marched into my room in descending order of importance, with Dr. Winn in the lead. I had not seen much of the man to whom I was deeply indebted. His unassuming manner touched me. On the bedside table stood a large jar filled with

M&Ms. It was labeled "Farkle Pills" and had been sent to me by the respiratory therapy students in my class at BSU. There was a long story behind the gift, and after his inquiry, I gave Dr. Winn an abbreviated version. He then popped a large handful of the candies into his mouth and ate them with relish. He said the sugar would pep him up for the next aneurysm case to which the phalanx of surgeons-in-the-making was en route.

Dr. Winn stringently adhered to the principle of patient confidentiality. He could tell that I was immediately drawn to the poor soul about to follow in my footsteps. He could give me no specifics but said the case would be a long and difficult one. A young fighter pilot from McChord Air Force Base had two aneurysms, one of which could not be clipped because of its location. The neurosurgeons would wrap that one in a special membrane. The clipping and wrapping would require complicated and dangerous intervention. Even as we spoke the operating room team was cooling down the jet jockey.

As the medical menagerie trickled out of the room I helped myself to some M&Ms. I thought often of the pilot as the evening progressed and sent up short prayers for his benefit. I struggled with my dinner tray while, three floors below me, the drama of Michael Robbins' life unfolded.

CHAPTER 15

AFTERMATH

While Michael's body was surrendering to the healing process in the caverns of Harborview, I continued in my struggle for autonomy on The Floor. Small accomplishments propelled me toward discharge. I could now bathe alone, albeit sitting down, and my walking path included several laps around the central nurses station. There continued to be minor glitches in my mental faculties and the telephone remained a mystery. I was still plagued by unpredictable temperature swings that produced an erratic pattern of donning and shucking clothing. The thermostat in the room ping-ponged between maximum and minimum.

The neurosurgeons, nurses, and therapists involved in my care decided that I was ready for discharge from the hospital although my destination remained undetermined. I had yet to conquer the mechanics of

108

swallowing to the speech therapist's satisfaction despite my dogged adherence to her schedule of tongue exercises and vocalizations. My generalized muscle weakness and left-sided impairment definitely needed some long-term intervention perhaps best handled in a rehabilitation facility.

As the collaboration among my medical caretakers continued, I reluctantly accepted the fact that I could not go home to Stanley, or even Boise. My fledgling confidence crumbled in light of the obvious fact that I could not yet take care of myself. At this time another ray of sunshine entered my life. Another prayer was answered.

My mother-in-law is a small woman whose nurturing character mirrors that of my mother. Shortly after my first operation Robert had put out an SOS call to his parents and "Miss Betty" responded in typical loving fashion. She arrived fully prepared to remain in Tacoma as long as necessary to get the Jarrett family through their crisis and Margaret back on her feet. She selflessly cooked meals, cleaned the house, did laundry, shored up Robert's sagging spirits, and helped Brian stay on track in school.

Because of Miss Betty's assistance I was able to be discharged much earlier than anticipated. I would be staying at Robert's house, thereby bypassing a transfer to Good Samaritan Hospital for rehab. I would receive ongoing outpatient speech, physical, and occupational therapies at MAMC at Fort Lewis. Miss Betty did more good for me than a dozen therapies.

On Wednesday afternoon May 7th I was wheeled around the nursing station to say my goodbyes. I dressed in a nightgown and robe and waited in a wheelchair by the elevator. I watched the other neurosurgery patients stagger past, pushing their walkers and IV poles. Some were slumped in wheelchairs along the walls with post-operative turbans wound around their heads. Some were drooling and muttering incoherently; they were far less fortunate stroke victims than I was. Some patients were strapped down on stretchers, obviously bound for other miseries elsewhere in the hospital.

After three weeks of self-centeredness, I was finally struck by a bolt of appreciation. I croaked out a long overdue prayer of thanksgiving as the elevator doors closed, removing me at last from The Floor.

Robert had little to say as we rode to the ground level. As he rolled the wheelchair out into a rare sunny spring day in Seattle his broad smile spoke more than words. He had prepared a bed for me in the back of the Tahoe. I muttered a prayer for fortitude as I crawled into the vehicle and tried not to retch as we wheeled away from Harborview's fortress-like west entrance.

I was going home! Instead of feeling elated I was fighting motion sickness and alternating between sweating and shivering. My considerate husband drove as steadily as possible and apologized for every pothole in the highway that he couldn't avoid. I could hear the whoosh of speedier traffic passing to our left and the ordinary sounds of people going about their business were soothing to my jangled nerves.

When we arrived at Robert's house in Lakewood I was determined to make it to the front door under my own power. Looking for all-the-world like an old crone, I hobbled to the entrance in my bathrobe and slippers. Miss Betty greeted me warmly as I collapsed on the living room floor practically in her lap. I stayed right there for the next two days as animated as a parsnip.

My futon and the paraphernalia of recovery converted our formal living room into a convalescent center. The presence of a wheelchair and a walker gave one the impression that an orthopedic casualty was in residence. Piles of pill containers, food trays, towels and tissue boxes completed the picture. My contribution to household affairs was to pop pills every four hours and shuffle to the bathroom.

I was able at last to talk to my mother on the telephone but I don't think she got much out of the conversation. My daddy was too ill for Mother to leave him, but her voice was thick with worry. Mother could hardly hear my croaky whispers. She finally had to get the full story from Robert. Other family and friends called with concerns and condolences but I avoided further conversations. I simply was not up to the task.

Miss Betty bustled around the house doing chores. She prepared soups and custards for me and standard fare for the guys. I drank gallons of Ensure. Robert bought a food processor and my selection of cuisine expanded to include pureed vegetables and meats which were a definite improvement over the jars of baby food.

I craved coffee and Miss Betty's morning brew smelled like a little bit of Heaven. In the hospital I had dreamed of sitting on the deck in the sunshine with a cup of coffee, just listening to the birds sing. At last I got to do just that. Never mind that I had on a heavy sweater with a dish towel over my bald head to protect it from the sun. It didn't matter that the coffee was only half a cup of decaf, or that I stayed outdoors only fifteen minutes. By the grace of God I was there, and the birds sang just as sweetly.

After I had spent several days on the living room floor it became obvious to all residents of the house that I needed to be upstairs in our bedroom and out of the way. Robert wanted to carry me up the short staircase but I insisted on going alone. I rolled my nightgown to my waist and stuffed it into my underwear. I sat down on the first step and scooted my rear end upward onto the second step while my family watched with apprehension. Robert hovered at the bottom of the stairs to catch me in case I lost upward momentum.

By the time I got to the landing my heart was pounding. After a long rest I crawled down the hall and into our bed with Robert's assistance. In spite of my exhausted trembling I was feeling pretty proud of myself. My husband relaxed a bit in his vigilance when he saw that my legendary stubbornness had returned with a vengeance.

Following my triumph over the staircase, life settled into a routine of sorts for the household. I still spent the majority of my time in bed and napped when I could. The days jumped around in fits and starts as if Tuesday couldn't find its way to Saturday in the proper sequence. I began listening to music although I could hear nothing in my left ear but a loud humming. The earphones felt strange since I still had no sensation of touch on the left side of my head.

Friends sent cassettes of mood music in hopes of improving mine, I suppose. My neck ached constantly and I could not get comfortable sitting or reclining. I had two enormous pills to coax down my throat every four hours to keep my blood pressure below boiling. I was on Dilantin for seizure prevention. Sleep continued to elude me. I was getting very grumpy.

Miss Betty never missed morning and afternoon snacks and the inevitable can of Ensure before bedtime. When I declared a permanent moratorium on Ensure, my resourceful mother-in-law substituted instant breakfast drinks and milk shakes. At the end of a week she had accomplished her goal of adding two pounds to my shrunken frame. We celebrated with a cup of real coffee. It was divine. It also sent my heart rate racing so Miss Betty restricted my daily caffeine intake to half a cup.

As my strength improved I was able to negotiate the stairs and began to join the family for evening meals. One night Brian ordered pizza. I experienced a profound wave of self pity as I sat at the dining room table and looked at my boiled zucchini and Gerber's strained turkey. I begged shamelessly until my husband let me have a tiny sliver of his slice of pepperoni. It tasted extraordinarily delicious but I had a major choking attack when a piece of crust lodged in the back of my throat.

The pizza episode ended my foray into solid foods for two weeks. Cookies and crackers soon joined the off-limits list. Because my tongue still deviated to the left and got in the way of chewing, most foods went down better if they could be slurped from a spoon or sucked through a straw.

Bathing was a rag job for the first week after my homecoming. My desire to be clean was overridden by my dread of the ordeal involved in becoming so. Robert surmounted this obstacle by buying a shower chair and firmly planting my uncooperative self on it under a steaming stream. He kept reminding me of how much better I would feel when my bath was finished. One more hurdle had fallen on the long road to my restoration.

Many unreasonable anxieties disturbed me. The baby steps of recovery included psychological victories as well as physical ones. I had persistent dyslexia for numbers which made it difficult for me to pay bills and keep track of fiscal matters regarding my home in Boise. Any checks I wrote had to pass Robert's inspection before they were mailed. A brief struggle with financial matters gave me a furious headache and drove me into a frustrated funk. Only my husband's gentle persistence kept my worldly affairs from falling into hopeless disarray.

I am by nature a very private person. The constant companionship necessitated by my illness made me feel smothered. The lack of privacy frequently embarrassed me. I was torn between the need for fellowship and the desire to be left alone. I was not above being petty and maudlin. My irritation must have been overtly obvious at times.

I am also not a patient person. I understood that the recovery process would be a slow one, and yet the exercises necessary for reconditioning muscles neglected for a month exhausted and annoyed me. How could I, who had been so physically fit, be such a wreck? Would I ever get back to normal? Despising my dependency gave me fuel for the fight to end it.

Robert often slept on a futon beside our bed as my restlessness interrupted his sleep. My obstinate refusal to take to sleeping pills and pain medication often deprived both of us of much-needed rest. As May grew warmer and the flowers proliferated my wounded body slowly healed.

Two marvelous people entered my life during this stage of recovery and improved my attitude. On May 14, one week after discharge from Harborview, I had my first follow-up visit at Madigan. Riding in a wheelchair and wearing a green felt hat, I rolled into the Family Practice clinic holding an ice pack to my face and clutching a can of Ensure. The other patients in the clinic failed to be impressed by the fact that I was being wheeled around the hospital premises by a colonel in full uniform.

Dr. Heidi Terrio was my assigned physician. After listening to a brief recapitulation of the long story of my mishap, she set about addressing my immediate needs for physical and speech therapies. She arranged appointments in the MAMC Neurology and Neurosurgery clinics and dismissed us quickly. I appreciated Dr. Terrio's brevity and her refusal to get bogged down in the complexity of my medical past.

I was paired with an energetic and handsome young physical therapist named Captain Maddox. He was a hard task master. He instantly surmised that I needed concrete goals and more than a little pushing. My devotion to Captain Maddox became a major motivator in the progress of my rehabilitation. I would have done a hundred repetitions of those monotonous exercises to win his approval.

By mid-June I was gaining weight and growing hair. I could prepare meals and complete simple projects. Miss Betty returned to her home in Oklahoma somewhat reluctantly. Perhaps she hesitated to condemn Robert and Brian to a life of my cooking. My husband ran errands and shopped and chauffeured with great forbearance. I was still struggling with numerical sequences and short-term memory loss. At least the telephone no longer stymied my communication with relatives and friends. Everyone I talked to said I was fortunate to have survived. I considered myself blessed rather than lucky.

By mid-July Tacoma was hot and humid. For the follow-up appointment with Dr. Winn I wore makeup and my best dress and spritzed my fuzz. I was surprisingly shy about meeting him. I had a vague recollection of our encounters in the hospital. In my neurosurgeon's office I was greeted warmly by a man much smaller than I remembered. He was not so tall after all. He had a weary gentleness underlying a prodigious intellect and a sense of humor that I had missed entirely.

Robert and I presented Dr. Winn with a jar of Farkle Pills and watched him promptly toss a handful into his mouth. His unhurried demeanor revealed not a whit of the incredible demands on his time. He was not concerned about my lingering left shoulder dysfunction and pharyngeal weakness. I think he was rather proud of his handiwork in a humble sort of way.

Dr. Winn scheduled a CAT scan for that afternoon to evaluate the persistent swelling beneath my left ear. We agreed on a return visit to his office in six months. When I questioned him about any restrictions on my activities my neurosurgeon gave a wry grin and asked, "Would it really matter even if there were?" And then I hugged him.

Robert and I had planned to spend the day in Seattle so we crossed the street to Harborview. He shared with me some of his memories of the hospital and my illness. We paused in the waiting room where my family had spent so many tortured hours. I peppered my husband with questions about how my cheering squad had passed the long anxious days.

We received permission to visit the Neurosurgical ICU. I wanted to see the room where I had suffered such torment and also had been the recipient of such miracles. I needed to set straight in my mind the orientation of the bed and equipment; the location of the clock I could not read; the television that was never turned on; to look at the great view I never saw. The blue walls and acoustical ceiling tiles were generic hospital decor and evoked no special recognition. The doors to the Trauma ICU were next to my room and I recalled their swinging and creaking ceaselessly.

Somehow I felt saddened by my tour of the Neuro ICU. Drs. Skirboll and Tandin had completed their training and moved on to positions in other hospitals. I would have liked to thank them. I wanted to tell Dr. Santiago how I had mistaken his gruffness for inconsideration but he was nowhere on the premises.

Robert and I left boxes of cookies for the ICU nurses and went to Three West. I felt even less connected to The Floor. Wheelchairs and walkers were scattered around and attested to the new wave of wounded. Beverly and Johnny were not yet on duty. We left more cookies and bid adieu to Room 314.

Then it was time for the CAT scan. It seemed strange to just walk down the hall in Radiology and climb up on the scanning table. After all, on my many previous trips I had been flat on my back. The room was as cold as I remembered it to be. I had a mild anxiety attack as the bed slid into the beehive-shaped scanner. I closed my eyes tightly and hummed Christmas carols, grateful that this time I was not strapped to the bed. The scan was quickly completed and I walked out with a little prayer that this might be my last appearance in Radiology. That was not to be the case.

Dr. Winn had arranged for us to review my ICU arteriograms with a radiologist. I finally got a good look at the little horror that almost killed me. It was bigger and uglier than I recalled from Peter's briefing in Boise. Robert and I were impressed by the markedly decreased cerebral blood flow evidenced on the set of arteriograms done three days postoperatively. My guardian angel had shown up in the person of Dr. Joe Eskridge with his miraculous skills at angioplasty. This was the perfect prelude to our scheduled appointment with the good doctor at the University of Washington.

After following a maze of hallways in the university's rambling hospital, we found the neuroradiologist in his tiny office at the end of the research wing almost buried by piles of x-rays, books and journals. Papers and boxes of catheters were stacked to the ceiling and falling over in places. We offered up thanks and more cookies and more hugs.

Dr. Eskridge proved to be a compassionate and unpretentious man who deserved all the praises my family had heaped upon him. He patiently demonstrated his technique for dilating the delicate vessels of a brain in vasospasm. I was in awe of this man who had meticulously manipulated tubes the size of pencil lead in the arteries of my head---this stranger who had intervened so profoundly on my behalf. My husband and I departed without adequate words of thanks.

Dr. Winn called a few days later with the result of the CAT scan. The large soft lump that had persisted behind my left ear was due to a meningocoele. This meant that a portion of my brain coverings had ballooned out through the surgical defect in my skull. Spinal fluid had accumulated beyond the squeezed-out portion and was now oozing between my neck muscles. No wonder my neck was so stiff and I couldn't get my head comfortable on a pillow.

Dr. Winn said it was possible that another operation would be required to close the meningocoele and perhaps even additional surgery to create an alternative path of fluid drainage. The very thought of undergoing major surgery again (especially so soon!) threw me into a fit of depression. I asked him if we could wait to see if the defect would improve on its own. Dr. Winn agreed that there was no serious risk in waiting. He instructed us to elevate the head of our bed as high as was bearable. He warned me to watch for signs of increased fluid pressure such as blurred vision or constant headache. I was crying by the end of the conversation and assured him that I would sleep sitting up if necessary.

Robert placed blocks under the headboard of our bed until we felt that we needed slings to sleep in. After sliding to the bottom of the mattress by morning, we compromised on a thirty-degree slant that was tolerable, though not comfortable, and stuck with it for three months. The lump slowly became smaller and firmer.

CHAPTER 16

MAKING LEMONADE

Colonel Robert Jarrett was the Chairman of the Department of Pediatrics at Madigan Army Medical Center. At the moment he was also serving, for a few days, as Acting Deputy Commander of Clinical Services at MAMC. In this capacity he was responsible for overseeing patient care and administrative issues for the hospital. For this reason he was currently sitting in the commander's morning report eating a Winchell's powdered sugar doughnut.

In addition to potential administrative headaches, the chiefs of all the clinical services discussed overnight admissions to the medical center's several intensive care units. On this particular morning toward the end of May, Colonel Jarrett learned of an admission to the surgical ICU that made him very happy. That may seem strange, considering that being admitted to intensive care is generally not looked upon as a happy occasion, but you shall see what I mean.

The Privacy Act forbidding disclosure of personal information outside of the medical center's purview prevented Colonel Jarrett from discussing, except in generic terms, this particular case which brought him a sense of gratitude as well as compassion. At the end of the day it was with a big grin on his face that he headed home to tell his wife.

At Fort Lewis we lived in a lovely old section of the base called Broadmoor. This was known as 06 housing, or Colonel's Quarters. It was a stately rectangle of well-kept lawns, large oak trees, and three-story brick homes where once President Dwight D. Eisenhower was housed. Broadmoor extended along the south side of the parade ground near the Commander's Circle, and the Jarretts considered themselves privileged to live there. We had recently moved on base from Lakewood to be nearer MAMC where Robert worked and I went regularly for rehabilitation services.

Cooking cannot be included in the list of my favorite domestic chores. I was engaged in a dutiful if somewhat futile attempt to prepare dinner when my husband walked into the kitchen and exclaimed, "You're never going to believe who's been admitted to the ICU at Madigan!"

Instantly alarmed, I quickly ran through the names of our small circle of friends, assuming that a tragedy had descended upon one of them. Robert shook his head in response to each name. Exasperated, I finally demanded that he divulge his secret. "Your jet jockey," he said with a smile, "from Harborview."

Colonel Robbins was back at MAMC after three weeks of being incised and revised, probed and reconstituted---a product of the miracle of modern medicine. His lithe figure was now gaunt, and dark stubble was showing up unevenly on his head. His tracheostomy was healing and covered with a square white "napkin." By plugging the hole he could converse briefly in a hoarse whisper. He accepted his impediment, believing it to be only temporary.

Maria came from Minnesota to be with her friend whenever possible. She noted Mike's absolute insistence on rapid improvement and felt that he actually willed his body to recover. Some cognitive deficits were noticeable, especially to her, attuned as she was to such, but they seemed minor in light of the enormity of his insult. It was Mike's short-term memory that appeared most affected, especially for names and places.

After three additional weeks of hospitalization at MAMC, the officer was discharged home with a litany of exercises, tracheostomy care protocols, special menus, and Dilantin. He was to be followed daily by home-health-care nurses and weekly by therapists at Madigan. His first homecoming was to last less than eight hours.

In order for Mike to bypass placement in an extended care facility, his family had agreed to week-long stints as his caretakers. Mandy had the first shift and was appalled to see her father stagger up the stairs and collapse in his bedroom. "Dad, you should still be in the hospital!" she cried with dismay. She was right. He was returned to Madigan via ambulance and spent another night receiving intravenous fluids for dehydration.

Back home again the jet jockey settled into a routine of sorts under Mandy's watchful eyes. Before the father left the house, the daughter checked out his ensemble as he was apt to leave zippers open and shoes untied and shirts buttoned crookedly. Since he had lost more than twenty pounds Mike's clothing hung on him like a coat on a rake. He maintained a serviceman's pride in his appearance despite the battered condition of his body.

As daughter was succeeded by son and father and Maria, the pilot progressed through the inventory of pureed produce and Gerber products to soft foods and the ubiquitous Ensure. Under the tutelage of a speech therapist Mike learned to use an electronic voice amplifier to enhance his soft whisper. This allowed him to talk on the telephone at last to his mother whose own health issues precluded her visiting her ailing son.

Mike's tracheostomy was to last for five months until his obsessive insistence upon decanulation led his physicians to remove it on a trial basis. Without the plastic prong in his throat the colonel felt free at last. But his vocal cord problems were far from over.

With the help of a walker the pilot could move around his small home and ambulate to his many therapy sessions. He struggled to re-master grooming and dressing skills. He was not allowed to drive for three months while he was still taking Dilantin. When Maria was available to chauffeur, she noticed that her friend's sense of direction, which had always been flawless, seemed to have deserted him. She gradually became comfortable taking charge of affairs that had previously been Mike's automatic responsibility. Maria did not object to the role reversal—it put a new spin on their relationship. In his turn, Mike learned to relinquish control and found his companion very capable indeed.

The pilot dutifully returned to Dr. Newell's office every three months for check ups. His brain MRI in October was normal. Other than numbness of his scalp and a stiff neck, he felt good. The only blank spot in his life was the huge portion formerly devoted to flying, and he missed it sorely. As soon as he was medically released to return to work, the jet jockey asked to be reassigned to flight status. The reappointment would prove to be anything but simple.

Because Mike had sustained a significant head "injury" with periods of unconsciousness and a seizure, the Washington ANG required an in-depth evaluation of his mental and physical capabilities. He would have to re-establish his proficiency in piloting. All of his fine-tuned skills and reaction times would be put through rigorous inspection. The pilot plunged into testing with a fervent desire to return to flying.

In March, 1998, Dr. Bottini found the pilot free of cognitive defects and with normal visual acuity and color vision. Nevertheless, the physician had ongoing concerns and recommended restriction against flying high-performance aircraft, which obviously included the Phantom and the Viper.

Colonel Robbins had another MRI at Harborview in April. Once again it was normal as was his neurological assessment by Dr. Newell. The neurosurgeon judged him fit to fly except under circumstances of high G-forces—namely, those found in fighter jets!

In July Mike's assessment at Camp Murray was again normal. The pilot's' evaluators felt that he still did not meet the standards for Class I flying rating despite his more than 2,700 hours of flight time. The same concerns about high gravity forces against his helmet and posterior neck region were again expressed. The jet jockey remained grounded.

At the beginning of his quest for restoration of his prior flight status Colonel Robbins was totally focused on the goal of getting back into the front seat of his beloved aircraft. As the weeks passed into months the pilot phased through difficult stages of frustration and denial. He gradually made peace with his earth-bound future as the realization of his true good fortune finally dawned on him. After all, he had backed away from the fine line and was being given a second chance for a new life that could be as rosy as he chose to make it.

In November a battery of neuropsychological tests was administered to the pilot at MAMC. The colonel's performances were well above average in all areas except for verbal learning trials. He seemed to have mild cognitive difficulties in verbal memory and information processing speed. Even Mike had noticed a disturbing tendency to get distracted easily. The end results were the same: no high-G environment; no solo piloting.

Maria continued to spend as much time with Mike as possible. His gentle and gentlemanly personality remained unchanged. In fact, his new willingness to let her assume responsibility for daily activities was endearing. Even though flying appeared to be only a part of his past, the pilot settled into a life of administrative work without a whimper. If he terribly missed flying, the colonel never showed this loss to family or colleagues. When handed a very large lemon in life, it seemed that Mike had decided to make lemonade.

CHAPTER 17

RESIDUE

The southern portion of Puget Sound narrows to a deep channel and then fans out into a series of fingers before disappearing below the city of Olympia. On opposite sides of the Sound the permanently grounded jet jockey and the retired pediatrician struggled to reconnect to lives momentarily left behind. They had no one with whom to share their experience who really understood what they had been through. But that situation was about to change.

In October the Olympia Yacht Club threw its annual Military Appreciation Day, called a FOOFARAW, at the Lucky Eagle Casino on the Sound. The Thurston County Chamber of Commerce joined in to make the event memorable for the two hundred mixed military personnel who received invitations. Colonel Michael Robbins was among them. So was Colonel Robert Jarrett.

Following an afternoon of games and fellowship and a marvelous seafood banquet, the men and women were returning to Olympia in small groups on private yachts. The ANG man was sitting on the bridge answering questions about his flying status when the Army man overheard him mention an aneurysm. My husband then uncharacteristically interrupted the ongoing discussion. He made no attempt to keep the excitement out of his voice as he asked, "Were you a patient at Harborview in the spring?"

"Yes!" the pilot answered affirmatively, slightly taken aback by the enthusiastic intrusion of his military counterpart. The two colonels took over the conversation.

Robert returned home in the late evening after the FOOFARAW and pulled his customary guessing game with me. When I heard that he had found the jet jockey once again, I knew that their meeting had not taken place by chance. Having both been touched by the same rough fingers of fate, the officer and I were meant to connect by some power beyond us.

I was nervous about meeting Colonel Robbins at Shenanigan's Restaurant on Ruston Way in downtown Tacoma. I had never been the least bit shy about meeting strangers before, but this encounter seemed, I don't know, so *intimate* somehow. Waiting for me in the lobby was a tall thin handsome man with a very short haircut. He was attired in dress blues uniform with silver eagles on the shoulders and looked every inch an officer and a gentleman. We shook hands solemnly and then the pilot leaned over and gave me a gentle hug.

In the months following his ruptured aneurysm, the

aviator without wings had to cope with problems that made mine seem minor by comparison. After many months of apparent good health he began having bouts of shortness of breath. At first his breathing restriction occurred only when he was exercising, but later it began to interfere with his daily activities. The vocal cord paralysis was exacting its toll on his airway at last.

After undergoing a series of tests at MAMC again, Mike was evaluated by an ear, nose, and throat specialist. In September, 1998, Dr. Goco cut a small wedge out of Mike's left vocal cord, enlarging his airway at the expense of his voice. Over time the officer's voice returned but so did the reduction in air entry. He was referred to the University of Washington Medical Center where Dr. Hillel reached the same conclusion. A repeat partial resection one year later again resulted in temporary improvement. Within months Colonel Robbins found himself in the same predicament---hoarse and short of breath with exertion. The ANG officer would find it difficult to be a commander without a voice, so he chose to live a life of restricted activity in exchange for the ability to communicate. In short, he was still making lemonade.

Had Colonel Robbins' aneurysm experience changed his life? He said, with a sense of wonder, "My whole life was a checklist! I was completely multi-tasked and goal-oriented. I compartmentalized my work and my play and my relationships. I could totally zero in on a problem and solve it, to the exclusion of all else. I think this ruptured aneurysm was God's way of telling me that I was *too* focused."

Maria agreed that her friend had changed in ways

she found appealing. He was less compulsive and more empathetic. He was a better listener. He seemed more comfortable expressing emotions and showing affection. Perhaps his behavior, honed to an edge in the military environment, was mellowing with age and hardships. When I put it to him that way, Mike laughed in his soft voice and said, "I am a very lucky person."

The colonel and I met occasionally for lunch both to commiserate and to work on this book. We formed a close bond of friendship while our authorial endeavor gave us a great excuse to try out some of the nifty restaurants in Tacoma. As we struggled to commit our thoughts and emotions to paper, Mike and I became increasingly aware of the gifts bestowed upon us by our Creator. We worked hard to rehabilitate our bodies while our minds curled themselves around the acknowledgement of our salvation.

AFTERWORD

Mike's lemons have been a lot bigger than mine. With an intense appreciation of the alternative, the colonel accepted an assignment to a desk job at McChord Air Force Base and retired from the Air National Guard with honors in 2005. His thin frame accumulated a healthy layer of flesh as he adjusted to a life of limited physical activity. His raspy voice and rapid breathing did not curtail his enjoyment of traveling and family affairs. Maria and Mike were married in 2003 with full understanding of what could have been the outcome of a ruptured aneurysm. They have embarked on major home improvement projects and remain grateful for each day they have together.

The residue from my ordeal has settled over my life very lightly. My major physical impediment is a neck filled with aches and stiffness. Like Colonel Robbins I must twist my torso to glance over either shoulder. Backing up a vehicle can be downright uncomfortable.

Three non-functioning muscles in my left shoulder and chest do not prevent me from shrugging into my heavy backpack at every opportunity. In April of 2003 I climbed to an altitude of 21,000 feet on the north side of Mount Everest. As I gazed across the high plateau of Tibet, stark in its pre-monsoon brownness, I was struck by a renewed appreciation of how blessed I have been. My husband and daughters continue to be the focal points of my life, but I often embark on solo adventures just for the sheer joy of living.

My bout with vocal cord paralysis has left me a bit hoarse. My voice has taken on a high-pitched timbre that surprises me when I hear it on the telephone answering machine. I have a propensity to choke on crumbly foods and must watch out for those crackers in my backpack. The mental fuzziness surrounding numbers persists and I suspect this deficit would have grounded me from the practice of Neonatology had I not already been retired from my medical profession.

High blood pressure had never been one of my worries prior to my ruptured aneurysm. In fact, my youthful athletic heart had maintained its slow rate and high stroke volume well into my middle adult years. Following surgery and vasospasm, however, hypertension is to be my companion from now on. I have joined the ranks of millions of hypertensive patients who regularly take their beta blockers and calcium channel blockers and diuretics. Hefty doses of ACE (angiotensin converting enzyme) inhibitor keep my blood pressure under reasonable control but leave me prone to violent episodes of coughing.

My handwriting, which was always legible but never neat, has deteriorated significantly. I sometimes find myself staring at the pen in my hand in a state of stupefaction, never knowing just how the word I am writing will turn out. My signature is now a sloppy scrawl applied with the same graceful flourish with which I might wield a hatchet.

As for the cabin in Stanley, I returned for the first time since my ordeal in September of 1997. Stepping onto that dreadful shag carpet brought only a sense of joy and freedom as I surveyed the scene of so much anguish. With a beatific smile at my husband I strode across the main room onto the front porch and checked the temperature.

ANGEL NOTES

I have discovered that many people seem uncomfortable discussing angels and near-death experiences if they have not personally encountered such phenomena. To me these events were uncomplicated and wondrous occurrences. I am simply an ordinary person to whom something extraordinary happened. I am still on this earth today because I have been gently touched by the hand of God.

Friends have questioned my angel visitations with expressions of both wonder and doubt. My experience was intensely personal but not unique. Angels are everywhere. I believe that they are a form of divine intervention in our lives.

Angels are summoned by prayer and often appear to rescue us from danger. They may show up at our side simply to give us safe passage through a rough spot in life. Children seem to possess a quality of acceptance that allows them to see angels very clearly.

An angel may take the form of a stranger who offers us assistance in a time of difficulty. One may appear out of the spiritual ether embodied in a close

134

acquaintance. I experienced both of these encounters ten days after my discharge from Harborview.

Dr. Winn had given me permission to fly home to Boise to attend Hiliary's graduation from Capital High School. He assured me that the clips on my aneurysm would not pop off with pressure changes during the flight! Family members escorted me in a wheelchair through the coliseum at Boise State University. A few eyebrows were raised as I glided toward the elevator wearing a heavy jacket in June and my dependable felt fedora. My daughter walked across the stage for her diploma just before my stamina gave out.

On the Sunday following graduation day I had recuperated sufficiently to attend worship services at First Presbyterian Church in Boise where I had been a member since 1984. For unexplained reasons I felt a compelling need to be at the eleven o'clock service despite my debilitated condition. As I moved slowly down the left aisle of the sanctuary and took my customary place at the end of the third pew, our analytically-minded minister, Mark Davis, spied my felt-hat-covered presence. His countenance lit up with a broad smile of joy and compassion as he made a direct line through the congregation in my direction.

With a matching smile of my own I stood to shake Mark's hand. Instead he wrapped his long arms around me in a tight embrace of Christian love. I felt a wave of intense warm energy flood my being as the healing power of God reached down through Pastor Davis and healed my wounded body. An angel had been at work.

Following the closing hymn of the morning service, a slender woman about sixty years of age, whom I had never before seen, approached me from two pews behind where I had been seated. Without a word of introduction or explanation she ran a soft warm hand along the blazing scar across the back of my head. She then turned her back and lifted her long graying hair, revealing a well-healed scar of almost exact same dimensions as mine. Smiling gently the woman leaned over and whispered, "We aneurysm survivors have much to be thankful for, don't we?"

I believe that angels are with us during our last moments in this world. They will appear to offer comfort as we cross the fine line from living into death. I know from my experience that I won't be making that crossing alone.

There is an understanding and a shared hope among those of us who have had a near-death encounter. It is something we cannot adequately explain except to each other. Even though the event differed for each of us survivors, we all felt a serenity that defies description.

For me death is no longer an unknown. I have reached a comfort zone with my mortality. I have been very near the final fine line at the edge of eternity. Now I understand the peace that surpasses all understanding. God is much closer. Heaven is much nearer.

BIBLIOGRAPHY

Ester Yarber and Edna McGown. *Stanley-Sawtooth Country*. The Caxton Printers, Ltd. Caldwell, Idaho. 1976. Reprinted by Publishers Press, Salt Lake City, Utah. 1998

Edna McGown. *The Far Side of the Mountain*. Edna McGown, Twin Falls, Idaho. 1983

Steve Fishman. *A Bomb in the Brain*. Charles Scribner's Sons, New York. 1988

Robert H. Wilkins, M.D. and Setti S. Rengachary, M.D., Editors. Aneurysms and Subarachnoid Hemorrhage. *In* Neurosurgery. Second Edition, Vol.II, Section C. New York, McGraw-Hill Companies, Inc. pp 2191-2276. 1996

Ronald D. Miller, M.D., Editor. *In* Anesthesia. Fifth Edition, Vol.II. London, Churchill Livingstone. pp 1913-1915. 2000

Julian R. Yousmans, M.D., Ph.D., Editor. *In* Neurological Surgery. Third Edition. Philadelphia, W.B. Saunders, Co. pp 1764-1806. 1990

Printed in the United States
80559LV00001B/88-135